A TRUSTED FRIEND

WHEN IT MATTERS MOST

RESPONDING
WITH
WISE COUNSEL

TIM CLINTON AND PAT SPRINGLE

LifeWay Press®
Nashville, TN

ISBN 9781415857328
Item 005089098

This book is a resource in the Personal Life category of the Christian Growth Study Plan.
Course CG-1101

Dewey Decimal Classification Number: 158.3
Subject Heading: FRIENDSHIP \ PEER COUNSELING \ HELPING BEHAVIOR

To order additional copies of this resource: write to
LifeWay Church Resources Customer Service; One LifeWay Plaza; Nashville, TN 37234-0113
fax (615) 251-5933; phone toll free (800) 458-2772; order online at *www.lifeway.com;*
e-mail orderentry@lifeway.com; or visit the LifeWay Christian Store serving you.

Printed in the United States of America

Leadership and Adult Publishing
LifeWay Church Resources
One LifeWay Plaza
Nashville, Tennessee 37234-0175

CONTENTS

Meet the Authors 5

Introduction 6

Week 1: Caring for Hurting People 9
    The Privilege of Being Used by God
    A Look Beneath the Surface
    The Responsibility of Trusted Friends
    The Biblical Basis of Trusted Friends
    The Goal of Trusted Friends
    Foundational Principles
    Characteristics of Trusted Friends
    Scope and Limitations
    The Vine

Week 2: Showing We Care 29
    The Role of Your Pastor
    A Short-Term Model
    Previewing the Process
    Care in Times of Crisis
    Care as Discipleship
    Common Misconceptions
    Eight Keys to Helping Wounded People
    God's Call

Week 3: Becoming a Great Listener 47
    Longing to Feel Heard
    Complexities of Communication
    Listening Skills
    A Touch of Humility
    Confidentiality
    Pay Attention to God As You Listen
    Listen Often, Listen Well

Week 4: Relying on the Scriptures and Prayer 67
Context and Permission
The Call to Honesty
The Need for Objectivity
Biblical Insights
Who We Are in Christ
The Importance of Prayer
Patterns of Prayer
Sharing the Good News
Representing God

Week 5: Providing Referral Sources 85
Common Problems
When and How to Refer
Establishing a Resource Network
Using the Network Effectively
The Matthew 18 Model
Boundaries
Some Difficult Issues
Caring for God's Flock

Week 6: Getting Started 107
Case Studies
Are You Ready?
Completing Referral Sources
Limitations
Go and Overflow

Appendix 119
Traditions of Christian Care
Stages of Grief
Passages of Encouragement and Hope
Why People Struggle and Suffer
Critical or Chronic Illness
Limits of Confidentiality

ABCs of Salvation 142

Leader Guide 143

Christian Growth Study Plan 157

Memory Verse Reproducible Worksheet 159

Notes 160

MEET THE
AUTHORS

TIMOTHY CLINTON, Ed.D., LPC, LMFT, an internationally recognized leader in Christian counseling today, is president of the nearly 50,000-member American Association of Christian Counselors (AACC), the largest and most diverse Christian counseling organization in the world. A licensed professional counselor and marriage and family therapist, Tim is the Executive Director of the Center for Counseling and Family Studies at Liberty University and is Professor of Counseling and Pastoral Care. Tim and his wife Julie live in Forest, Virginia, with their two children, Megan and Zach. Tim has authored more than 150 articles and numerous books including *Why You Do the Things You Do: The Secret to Healthy Relationships; Loving Your Child Too Much: How to Stay Close without Overindulging, Overprotecting, or Overcontrolling; Turn Your Life Around: Breaking Free from Your Past to a New and Better You;* and is the executive editor of the newly released *Bible of Hope.*

PATRICK SPRINGLE, MA in Counseling, is president of Baxter Press. Pat has been a leading writer and conference trainer in support group ministries, having authored such materials as *Untangling Relationships* and *Conquering Codependency.* Previously Pat served on the staff of Campus Crusade for Christ as the Texas state director and as vice president of Rapha Treatment Centers, a hospital-based Christian counseling program. Baxter Press works with Christian organizations to publish materials for their constituents. Pat and his wife Joyce live in Friendswood, Texas. They have two children, Taylor and Catherine, and a son-in-law, Paul.

A TRUSTED FRIEND
INTRODUCTION

Being a member of a church is one of the greatest adventures in life. We become a part of a family—God's family—because God designed the church as a place for brothers and sisters in Christ to receive the fellowship and encouragement of others.

Whether you realized it or not, you have entered a partnership with God in touching the lives of men and women, young and old, who need to experience God's kindness, wisdom, and strength. We all know people who are hurting from past and present wounds. It's hard to lose a parent or child ... to battle cancer ... to have kids who think you are the worst parent in the world ... to face bills when you don't have enough money to pay them ... to grow up without a dad ... to face the guilt of a past abortion ... to be abused by someone you loved and trusted. And many of us have experienced these same wounds ourselves. But we need to offer more than sympathy and compassion. We need to be prepared to share with others the hope and healing we found in Christ.

Many of you are already known for your compassion and care, so this training will provide additional insights, skills, and resources to help you become even more effective. Perhaps in the past you've not felt competent to deal with those in crisis or ongoing problems, but now you want to learn these skills. Welcome to this study. We believe you can be a trusted friend to family, church members, coworkers, neighbors, and others God has placed in your life.

People around us try to hide their hurts, but if we look closely, we'll notice the evidences of their pain, anger, or fear. If we take time to look behind the eyes of other people into their hearts, chances are we'll find hurting people.

What do hurting people do with their pain? Some of them try to:
- press on, as if nothing is wrong and hope that if they keep their eyes closed long enough, the pain will go away;
- cry and beg God for relief but still feel hopeless;
- intimidate others to gain power over them;
- please everyone to earn their love;
- fill the hole in their hearts with financial success;
- numb the pain with drugs, alcohol, gambling, food, or sex.

It's no wonder that Solomon wrote, "A happy heart makes the face cheerful, but heartache crushes the spirit" (Prov. 15:13).

Whatever the struggle, God assures us that we are never alone. He doesn't promise a problem-free life, but He assures us there will be no storm too great, no load too heavy, or any distance too long. In every circumstance He is present, and He can use even the most painful moments in our lives to deepen our trust in Him and to give us more compassion for others who hurt like we do (or have been hurt).

God's plan to give hope and direction to those who struggle involves people like you who become His voice, His arms, and His feet to carry and communicate His love to hurting people. In fact, He delights in using us to give hope to the hopeless, direction to the lost, and strength to those who feel weak. We have the unspeakable privilege of communicating grace and truth to people in the most vulnerable moments of their lives—as Christ does. Read these prophetic words about the Messiah:

> The Spirit of the Lord GOD is on Me,
>> because the LORD has anointed Me
>> to bring good news to the poor.
>> He has sent Me to heal the brokenhearted,
> to proclaim liberty to the captives,
>> and freedom to the prisoners;
>> to proclaim the year of the LORD'S favor,
>> and the day of our God's vengeance;
>> to comfort all who mourn,
> to provide for those who mourn in Zion;
>> to give them a crown of beauty instead of ashes,
>> festive oil instead of mourning,
>> and splendid clothes instead of despair.
>> And they will be called righteous trees,
>> planted by the LORD,
>> to glorify Him (Isa. 61:1-3, HCSB).

Highlight or underline key words or phrases that you think describe a trusted friend.

Expectations for the Next Six Weeks

You are about to begin a six-week journey that will *intellectually*, *emotionally*, and *spiritually* prepare you to care for people more effectively. The topics in our study will help you identify needs by listening to people carefully, encouraging them with your compassion, and directing them to competent professional resources. Don't expect to be perfect at these tasks … ever. And don't expect to be able to help everyone in every situation. Not even Christ helped everyone who crossed His path in Palestine.

The best model of helping is Jesus Himself—the ultimate trusted friend—who combined compassion, knowledge, skill, the Spirit's power, integrity, and strong relationships. He was *compassionate* with others by reaching out and touching outcasts, lepers, and other untouchables in that society. He challenged false beliefs and dark thoughts with His knowledge of the truth about the character and purposes of God.

He *skillfully* gave people life-changing hope in even the darkest moments of their lives. He promised rest and peace through the *Holy Spirit*. He modeled ethical *integrity*. And He involved others in the process of helping as they formed strong, loving *communities of care*.

Christian caring is wonderful, maddening, joyous work. As we walk with hurting people, we are sometimes overwhelmed, often confused, and always in awe that God would use us to touch others' lives at their points of need. We are, after all, well aware of *our own* needs for God's grace, mercy, and strength.

The wonder of it all is that Jesus sends His Spirit—all the time and in every way—to comfort us, fill us with His grace, and enable His love to overflow from us into the lives of those around us. Finding Him in the middle of every situation—and meeting Him in the middle of every need—is the source of our strength as we serve as trusted friends.

Trusted friends are found in your pastor and staff, deacons and wives, Sunday School officers and teachers, discipleship leaders, women's and men's ministries, prayer teams, and lay men and women who just know how to listen and care.

If you did not find yourself in this list, we've got great news. God will use this study to equip you for this ministry and your small group will continue to pray for you and share insights long after these six weeks are over. Out of your overflow of God's grace in your life, you will reflect Him as you serve God and others in a loving environment we call the church.

TIM CLINTON AND PAT SPRINGLE

week one

CARING FOR HURTING PEOPLE

"Praise be to the God ... who comforts us in all our troubles, so that we can comfort those in any trouble with the comfort we ourselves have received from God."

2 Corinthians 1:3,4

Day by day each of us needs a comforting word, an expression of caring, or the chance to have a listening ear. And we have those same opportunities with others. Even the Bible heroes had days of depression, guilt, or discouragement. When he wrote his psalms, King David was open about his personal struggles. In Psalm 51 he asked God to "wash away my guilt and cleanse me from my sin" (Ps. 51:3, HCSB). Most people don't feel comfortable sharing their personal problems with other believers. The underlying assumption is that all the other people at church are walking with God and have their acts together. I'm the only one who's struggling, so I'm going to keep my mouth shut.

That's certainly not the way God wants the church to function. (Besides, it's not a true reflection of the members.) He wants His people to focus on His goodness and greatness. They can find new hope in His plan for their lives and love so unlike the world that unbelievers would ask, "What makes those people so different?" (1 John 4:7-8).

THE PRIVILEGE OF BEING USED BY GOD

In spite of incredible advances in medicine and technology, the human condition isn't improving. We're just as selfish and sinful as ever. Those who touch the lives of people today see the statistics come to life in the hurting faces or devastated relationships caused by a host of evidence of the fallen nature of humankind. People around us—including some in our own families—are wounded and broken. God has put us in their lives, and we have both the high privilege and the responsibility to care about them.

Part of being real with God means that we come "just as we are"—not only when we first trust Christ but all day every day as believers. The church can be, as author and psychologist Larry Crabb has pointed out, "the safest place on earth" so that people feel comfortable opening their hearts to share their needs with one another.[1] Our model is Jesus, who displayed signs both of disappointment and anger (Matt. 23:37; John 2:14-17) and recognized them in others. His joy was to help the people around Him because He knew their wounds and compassionately met their needs.

Read the three lists, and check the problems you've noticed in your church family. Double check beside problems you've experienced.

- ❑ a death in the family
- ❑ an accident or critical illness
- ❑ the arrest of a teenager (or adult child, spouse, or parent)
- ❑ a marriage partner suddenly leaving

People you know may experience a sudden, unexpected crisis.
Or you may be dealing with long-term, chronic problems:

❑ the strain of a blended family
❑ depression
❑ chronic or terminal physical illness
❑ consuming debts
❑ prodigal children

People need support and encouragement in life stages such as:

❑ the empty nest
❑ single parents
❑ widows or widowers
❑ military families relocating again
❑ aging parents

Describe a situation when God used you to provide comfort,
support, and direction to a hurting person. (Come on, God gets
the glory. You're just recounting what He did through you.)

God did this through my life:

Trusted friends aren't always involved with wounded people or a life-or-death ministry.
Some problems in the church family—such as malicious gossip, disagreements, committee
infighting, stubbornness, opposition to change, jealousy, or selfishness—may seem small
by comparison, but they are just as real to the persons who are experiencing them. You'll
learn more about what we mean by being a trusted friend to hurting people as you study
during these next few weeks. We hope you will feel that you can use your abilities and past
experiences effectively. And, let's all admit it, we have problems too.

A LOOK BENEATH THE SURFACE

Mike taught an adult Sunday School class. Mike helped a member, Richard, whose relationship with his 20-year-old son was shattered. Through Mike's encouragement and guidance, Richard learned to listen to his son instead of constantly trying to control him. "I had trouble relating to my dad too," Mike remembered. "I only told my friend the things I wish my father had done in his relationship with me. And thankfully, God used the little knowledge I had to help a friend with one of the most painful relationships he had ever faced."

Christians certainly aren't immune to problems. We get sick and die at the same rate as unbelievers. Similar death rates are understandable. But we also have similar rates (or higher) of divorce, drug abuse, problems with food, gambling, and pornography. In a church setting, however, we usually see only surface symptoms of deeper problems, but these surface signals are often painfully apparent, such as:

- a look of discouragement
- snapping at children or others
- missing worship, groups, or classes
- complaining with passion about a relatively small matter

Of course many people experience the chronic strain of ongoing care for another person. And problems often come in clusters. For example, living with an addicted person almost necessarily involves hearing lies and being deceived. The addict spends a lot of money on his or her habit, so the family finances are often in shambles. The addict is out of control, and the whole family revolves around that person's lifestyle and attitude. Children are neglected or rigidly controlled, so they often act out in destructive ways such as eating disorders and bullying.

As we look beneath the surface of a discouraged look on a person's face, we may open a Pandora's box of trouble, or more likely, the discouraged person will try as hard as possible to keep the lid on and assure everyone that everything is "normal." Through authenticity, love, and persistence, we have to earn the right to be heard before the person will open up and begin to tell us what's wrong.

Being a trusted friend in these situations isn't a ministry for which you sign up. No long lines of people wait to apply. You find problems in your extended family, down the street where you live, in your Sunday School class, on your deacon ministry team roster, or on your church league baseball team. In some cases people will share what's going on in their lives whether we want to know or not! Or, we may perceive that a person has an issue bothering him or her. Before we intervene, we need to:

- ask for permission to get involved (May I ask you a personal question?)
- feel a sense of God's calling (God keeps putting this person on your mind.)
- have no hidden agendas ("People will like me, or I'll get attention if I help" is not an appropriate motive.)

On a scale of 0 (not at all) to 10 (completely), how safe do you think churches are for people to be honest about their hurts, disappointments, anger, or sinfulness?

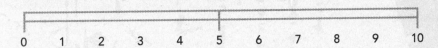

THE RESPONSIBILITY OF TRUSTED FRIENDS

Bill was at his wit's end. Ever since he married Jackie, she and Bill's sister Pam had gotten along like a balloon and a needle. As long as they didn't try to talk about anything important, they were cordial, but sparks flew at the slightest provocation. Bill tried to help them resolve their differences, but each time he brought it up to Jackie, she erupted. Pam refused to even discuss the problem.

Bill called Ralph, a long-time friend, for help. Ralph reminded him, "Bill, do you remember when I was so upset because my brother and my father got so mad at each other that they didn't speak for over a year?" Ralph could identify with Bill's situation, so he was able to help Bill unravel his own feelings of confusion and his resentment toward his sister and his wife. Ralph gave him some ideas about how to begin the process of building bridges between the two women.

Wounded people are fragile, vulnerable, and often brittle. They may have completely lost hope, or they may be defiant and angry with people and with God for allowing them to hurt so badly. They may be in shock from a traumatic event, or they may have experienced abuse or abandonment so long that their pain and loneliness has become "normalized." They simply don't know any other way to live. Self-protection is natural and expected, but it often compounds the initial problem.

On page 14 write signs that would indicate that someone has an emotional wound he or she is carrying around.

facial

gestures

posture

actions

Some self-medicate to numb the pain, and others participate in risky behaviors to try to fill the emptiness inside. Some people build high walls to keep people out while others try to control people and situations. People try to prove themselves to show they have value, and some seek to win the approval they desperately want by doing whatever they think will please other people. Many of those around us—including our own families—are wounded and broken. God has put us in the lives of hurting people, and we have both the high privilege and the responsibility to care for them.

Read John 17:22-23. Why is caring for people a "high privilege"?

Read Galatians 6:2 and 1 John 4: 11,21. Why is it a responsibility God has given you to fulfill?

Our responsibility is to look beyond the hopelessness, the anger, the walls, and the controlling behavior of hurting people to see their wounded hearts. Their outward behavior may be annoying, confusing, or repulsive, but if we look deeper, we'll see that God has made us all with a deep longing to love and to be loved. God gave us the privilege and responsibility to help uncover these needs and be a resource for God to touch lives with His grace, power, and love.

Many people experience the chronic strain of providing ongoing care to a needy person (for example, someone with a terminal illness or with mental or physical disabilities). Problems often come in clusters. For example, living with an addicted person almost necessarily involves hearing lies and being deceived.

The addict has spent a lot of money on his or her habit, so the family finances are often in shambles. The addict is out of control, and the whole family revolves around that person's lifestyle and attitude. Children are neglected or rigidly controlled so that they often act out in destructive or depressive ways.

As we look beneath the surface, we may open a Pandora's box of trouble, or more likely, the discouraged person will try as hard as possible as long as possible to keep the lid on and assure everyone that everything is OK. Through authenticity, love, and persistence, we have to earn the right to be heard before the person will open up and begin to tell us what's wrong.

As we try to help struggling and hurting people, what are some reasons it's important for us to be …

authentic

loving

persistent

THE BIBLICAL BASIS OF TRUSTED FRIENDS

Amy sent an e-mail to those who belonged to a cell group Bible study she attended. She was having a panic attack and pleaded for help from anyone who would respond. Betty had experienced panic attacks years before, so she knew the desperation Amy felt. She e-mailed her and helped calm her fears.

"I remember what it was like for me," Betty explained, "and I was happy to step in and help her get through that difficult moment."

We gain immediate insight into the value God places on caring for those in need when Jesus promised that the Holy Spirit, the Helper, and Comforter would come to guide His followers after His ascension. The very nature of God is both almighty and tender, far above all yet as near as our breath. In a beautiful description of the Messiah who would come, Isaiah quoted God saying:

> *"Here is my servant, whom I uphold,*
> *my chosen one in whom I delight;*
> *I will put my Spirit on him and he will bring justice to the nations.*
> *He will not shout or cry out, or raise his voice in the streets.*
> *A bruised reed he will not break, and a smoldering wick he will not snuff out"*
> *(Isa. 42:1-3a).*

Centuries later when this servant "became flesh and made his dwelling among us" (John 1:14), the Gospel writers gave us a clear picture of Christ's immense compassion. He befriended outcasts, tax gatherers, and prostitutes. He healed the sick, the lepers, the demon possessed, and the crippled, who were considered the dregs of society. When others expected Him to project an image of power and authority, He called little children to come to Him and told those around Him, "The kingdom of God belongs to such as these" (Mark 10:14).

How do you think the "dregs of society" felt when Jesus singled them out for attention and affection? Circle your choices.

surprised   unworthy   confused   grateful   embarrassed

offended   other? _____

In a striking depiction of the last judgment, Jesus said that a measure of our devotion to Him is shown in how we care—or fail to care—for those who are hungry, thirsty, sick, naked, and in prison. And Jesus takes our efforts personally. He said, "I tell you the truth, whatever you did for one of the least of these brothers of mine, you did for me" (Matt. 25:40).

Who are "the least of these" in your church and community?

What would you say to someone who voiced this common reaction: "Stay out of it. It's none of your business"?

For those who claim to know Christ, caring for those in need is not optional. His instructions to all of us are to "love one another," a directive He repeated many times (see John 13:34-35; 15:17). Jesus wasn't talking about only loving people who are easy to love. He told us to love our enemies, those who despitefully use us. The phrase, "turning the other cheek," has become a well-known and frequently quoted saying.

His example to love those who don't love us in return (Luke 6:32) measures our devotion and willingness to follow Him. The apostle Paul was known for his zeal and determination to take the gospel to the whole world, yet in his personal relationships this "tough guy" gave equal measures of tenderness and direction.

In the passage below, underline the words that indicate Paul was a trusted friend.

> *"But we were gentle among you, like a mother caring for her little children. We loved you so much that we were delighted to share with you not only the gospel of God but our lives as well, because you had become so dear to us."*

A few verses later, he wrote, *"For you know that we dealt with each of you as a father deals with his own children, encouraging, comforting and urging you to live lives worthy of God, who calls you into his kingdom and glory"* (1 Thess. 2:7-8,11-12).

Paul recognized that "one size doesn't fit all" people in all situations. Interaction with people must be tailored to the person and the moment. In the same letter, Paul instructed them, "And we urge you, brothers, warn those who are idle, encourage the timid, help the weak, be patient with everyone. Make sure that nobody pays back wrong for wrong, but always try to be kind to each other and to everyone else" (1 Thess. 5:14-15).

List some situations when someone we care about needs to be:

warned

encouraged

corrected

In the New Testament, all of us are called to serve God and one another. The Greek word for service, *therapeia,* indicates service given to people in times of turmoil. In this context, then, *therapy* is attentive, careful help for people in need.

Of course, Jesus Christ, the first and foremost example of someone who renders this kind of service, gave Himself to provide intimate, restorative, redemptive care to all people. The examples of Christ, Paul, and other biblical writers give us a firm foundation for a ministry of serving and caring for people who suffer or need other kinds of help.

Four New Testament passages (Rom. 12; 1 Cor. 12; Eph. 4; 1 Pet. 4) contain lists of spiritual gifts—abilities God has given to believers to equip them to serve more effectively. We can be sure that God has given each of us an ability He wants to use to extend His kingdom to all the world (Matt. 28:18-20).

Gifting, though, is only one component. As we listen to God's directives, each of us finds our specific calling to a place of service in the body of Christ. Our experiences—both successes and failures, good times and bad—also shape our lives, deepen our love for God, and give us empathy for the needy.

As stewards of all God has entrusted to us and of all our God-given abilities, we need to sharpen our skills so we are ready when the opportunity comes. In giving care for hurting people, most of us have a lot to learn! The complexities of personality, stages of life, strained relationships, finances, and other issues keep us humble and eager to learn.

Have you ever taken a spiritual gifts inventory? If so, what would you say are your spiritual gifts?

If not, talk to your group leader about taking an inventory.
Spiritual Gifts: A Practical Guide to How God Works Through You by David Francis is an excellent resource.[2]

What experiences and training—or talents and service—would give you insight to help a fellow church member?

THE GOAL OF TRUSTED FRIENDS

Kathy heard the news that Janet's husband had died of a heart attack just hours before. Kathy and Janet were supposed to be in a women's Bible study later that morning, but Kathy changed her schedule to go immediately to Janet's house.

When she walked in, Janet burst out in tears, "I'm so glad you're here. I feel so alone. Will and I are—were—so close, and now I feel like my heart has been ripped out." In the hours that followed that awful day and for the next few weeks, Kathy became a trusted friend who listened to Janet's hurts, found information she needed, and walked with her through her time of shock.

"I don't know what I would have done without you," Janet told her. Kathy just smiled and nodded. Although the experience was full of pain, she felt blessed to reach out to her friend with the hands and heart of God.

The goal of helping someone deal with a problem or problem person is not simply to relieve pain or "fix" the situation. Instead, the primary goal is helping each person become a fully devoted follower of Jesus Christ. C. S. Lewis said that pain is "God's megaphone" to get our attention so He can teach us valuable lessons. In many cases people refuse to listen to God's whisper and only hear Him when He uses the megaphone of pain in their lives.

Far too often, well-meaning friends tell people that God's goal is to relieve their pain, and they promise that God will cause their hurt to go away. Certainly God's plan is for each person to experience a life in all its fullness (John 10:10), but God's abundance isn't always pleasant. God's curriculum for all of us, at one time or another, involves times of pain, darkness, and waiting (see Heb. 12:2; Jas. 1:2).

J. I. Packer has written that when we promise more than God intends to deliver, we are "cruel" to our listeners because they assume that "God has let them down" when He doesn't deliver.[3] Those promises, then, are misleading and counterproductive. We might have good-hearted intentions to restore hope to needy people, but our motives do not make overpromising any less cruel.

Which statement(s) might indicate that you have overpromised what God will do in a given situation? Check one or more.

❑ I told Lucas he would get well.
❑ I just knew a job for Angela was right around the corner.
❑ I agreed with Harriet that Scott was the guy for her.

A proper understanding of the biblical principles of spiritual life imparts hope—real hope—to suffering people. This biblical hope is the foundation of genuine progress. One of our purposes in befriending others is to define, describe, and model the strong, life-changing hope we find in God.

If we are effective as trusted friends, what must be our motives?

What should be our goals?

FOUNDATIONAL PRINCIPLES

As you read these foundational principles, you will find they are absorbed best when they are discussed with your group. We suggest small groups, Bible studies, and training to reinforce and deepen understanding and application of these principles. In order to share and encourage others, you need a solid foundation on which to stand. Some of the principles that form a foundation for insight and growth include these.

1. We are loved and adopted by God.
   Loneliness and isolation form two of the chief problems for those who evidence a need for help. They need to be convinced that God is kind, attentive, and thrilled to have them as His own. One of the most important affirmations in our lives is to say to God, "I belong to You."

2. We can trust God because of His infinite greatness.
   God spoke and the stars were flung into space, and His majesty is beyond our wildest imaginations. We base our faith on equal parts of wonder at His transcendent greatness and amazement at His tender love.

3. God has called each of us to make a difference.
   Each of us has a role to play in God's purpose of redeeming men and women, and He invites us to be His partners in the greatest adventure ever known. Os Guinness wrote: "God calls us to himself so decisively that everything we are,

everything we do, and everything we have is invested with a special devotion and dynamism lived out as a response to his summons and service."[4]

4. Grief is a normal and healthy response to loss.

We live in an instant society, and many people expect complex problems to be resolved as quickly as the plot resolution in an hour-long television drama. But it doesn't happen that way in real life. Recovering from loss takes time, attention, and courage.

We usually think of grieving in connection with death, but processing and resolving pain involves grieving for any kind of loss, from mild to traumatic, both chronic and sudden. In fact, virtually every person who needs a trusted friend has experienced significant loss: disease, death, moving away from friends, prodigal children, strained or broken relationships, addictions, feelings of hopelessness, or rejection by friends. For many (if not most), unresolved losses in the past adds to their present hurt, so the pain is multiplied.

One of the most important ways we can help people is to walk with them through the process of grieving their losses. The appendix contains an explanation of the stages of grief, and we will begin to study this section in week 2.

5. God uses pain as a tool to shape our lives.

Oppressive pain paralyzes us. That kind of pain needs to be relieved so that we can think clearly. But once we reach that point, we need to learn from our pain instead of simply trying to avoid it. Recall the analogy that pain is God's megaphone to get our attention and God's hammer and chisel to form our lives the way He desires.

6. We need to assign appropriate responsibility for our pain and take the right action in response.

A victim mentality leads us to blame others for problems we have created and to blame ourselves for others' sins. Clarifying our responsibility helps us overcome paralyzing blame, self-pity, and passivity. We can then take strong action to change the direction of our lives, set appropriate limits, and fulfill God's call.

7. Our strong hope is in the presence and purposes of God.
    There are times when both the presence and the purposes of God seem clouded or nonexistent, but even then we can trust that He is at work through our struggles, to accomplish His divine purposes. We will never get to a point that we no longer feel pain. In this life, we groan, longing to be with God (see Rom. 8:23). But struggle and pain are not the enemy; they are God's tools to draw us to Him and to shape our desires and values so that we want what He wants.

Review these principles; then put the number of the principle that applies to you in the blanks.

Which principle has God used most powerfully to comfort you? ____

Which has encouraged your faith in Him? ____

Which do you need to develop to be a trusted friend? ____

Which of these principles seems most difficult to apply? ____

What are some practical ways you can impart these principles to those you care for? Respond to at least three of the four.

through my words

through sharing my losses

through my emotions

through my faith

CHARACTERISTICS OF TRUSTED FRIENDS

In week 1 you've read the stories of real people in need of caring friends. Review these stories. Did you see yourself in any of these situations? If so, which one(s)? Underline your answers.

Mike and Richard   Amy and Betty

Bill and Ralph   Kathy and Janet

Which of these would describe you?

❏ uncomfortable being with a hurting person
❏ "been there, done that"
❏ unsure as to what to say
❏ confident and caring
❏ willing to be trained to be a trusted friend to others

In his classic book, *The Wounded Healer,* Henri Nouwen wrote that only those who have been wounded themselves can identify with others who hurt. Wounded healers can then comfort others with the comfort they have received from God (2 Cor. 1:4). If you have been wounded and restored, don't think those wounds are useless or just bad memories. God wants you to redeem those experiences by helping others through those same mine fields. Other characteristics include:

• **Personal maturity:** Helping people in need is stressful, so trusted friends must be emotionally stable and strong. If their own unresolved wounds cloud their care, they will use other's problems to resolve their own issues instead of focusing on the needs of others. People whose wounds are still fresh may be compassionate and empathize easily with hurting people, but they need to take a few steps farther down the path of healing and growth before they dive headlong into ministering to those with fresh grief.

• **Spiritual maturity:** The goals of a trusted friend aren't simply to relieve pain. Instead we strive to help each person process their emotions, behaviors, and relationships and learn important lessons about dependence on God. This clear and powerful perspective needs to be combined with a working knowledge of Scripture (finding and explaining passages that accurately address situations) and a vital prayer life (tapping into God's resources and guidance). We must avoid magical thinking that everything will work out like we want because we prayed.

- **Gifts and desire:** The easiest way for a person to know if he or she has been equipped by God for any role is the affirmation of others. If they say, "You are terrific at listening to people, understanding their problems, and pointing them in the right direction," that's a good sign that the person has the gifts and calling to be a trusted friend. Such people usually experience a genuine delight when God uses them to help a hurting person. That delight fuels their desire to help even more people.

- **Time:** Caring for people requires us to be available when a crisis occurs or the person wants to talk. Listening is demanding work, so we need adequate time, energy, and focused attention.

- **Teachable spirit:** All of us are in process. Human nature is exceedingly complex, and family relationships are often complicated. As caring friends we need to learn more about the Scriptures, applications to specific situations, resources we can use, and other information that will help us care more effectively.

Rate yourself from 0 (nonexistent) to 10 (fully competent) for each of these areas:

____ Life experience of woundedness   ____ Teachable spirit

____ Personal maturity   ____ Spiritual maturity

____ Gifts and desire   ____ Time

Based on this assessment, what are your strengths as a trusted friend?

In what areas do you need more training or resources?

SCOPE AND LIMITATIONS

At the end of this training, you will not be a counselor. You will not have the education, the training, the supervised practicum, the skills, or the license to provide professional care. However, you will understand how to identify needs and find appropriate resources to meet those needs. And with those skills, God will use you to transform lives.

To help you know what to expect in this training, look carefully at this overview.

- In week 1 we've given you a summary of the motivations and biblical basis for trusted friends. We've listed some of the needs and situations where this care can be helpful in your church and your community, and we've outlined the characteristics needed for this ministry.

- Week 2 will explain how to honor the position of your pastor and/or staff by knowing how they function when a problem or problem person comes to their attention. You may find that you are a help or a hindrance to what they are doing. We will give you a four-step model of befriending others in more detail, along with other factors that you may encounter such as how people grieve.

- Week 3 outlines practices and techniques to focus on listening skills, a vital element for anyone who wants to be of help to others.

- Week 4 explains the power of God's Word and the importance of prayer as we serve as trusted friends to those in need.

- Week 5 explores the necessity of identifying local professional counselors, support groups, government agencies, and other organizations that can provide important resources for people in need.

- Week 6 covers a wide range of case studies that will help you practice the skills you have acquired, find help for caregivers, and know practical suggestions for getting started or taking the next step in this ministry. You will complete your referral directory.

Caring about people in need is one of the most challenging activities in life. When we sense that God uses us to help an individual or a family deal with a crisis or a long-term problem, we feel like Eric Liddell in *Chariots of Fire* when he explained to his sister why he was determined to participate in track at the Olympics. She couldn't understand her brother's devotion to the sport, but he put his hands on her shoulders and said, "Jenny, Jenny. God made me fast, and when I run, I feel his pleasure." When you and I run the race of restoring hope to the hopeless, we too will feel God's pleasure. And that's enough.

In what personal ministry situations do you feel God's pleasure?

Who are some people you know right now who need a trusted friend?

Complete this statement: A few months after I've taken this training, I hope God is using me to

Take some time to pray. Ask God to equip you and others in your training group so you can represent Him with grace and strength.

Dear God,

THE VINE

We're sure you've noticed the vines on each week's introduction page. We couldn't think of a more appropriate visual to encourage trusted friends. Read John 15:1-5.

> "I am the true vine, and my Father is the gardener. He cuts off every branch in me that bears no fruit, while every branch that does bear fruit he prunes so that it will be even more fruitful. You are already clean because of the word I have spoken to you. Remain in me, and I will remain in you. No branch can bear fruit by itself; it must remain in the vine. Neither can you bear fruit unless you remain in me. I am the vine; you are the branches. If a man remains in me and I in him, he will bear much fruit; apart from me you can do nothing."

We must never lean on our personality, skills, or knowledge as we help people in need. Each time you see these vines throughout your member book, let them remind you of your reliance on Jesus Christ, the One who gives you wisdom, strength, and direction.

---

1. Larry Crabb. *The Safest Place on Earth* (Nashville, TN: W Publishing Group, 1999), 8.

2. David Francis. *Spiritual Gifts: A Practical Guide to How God Works Through You.* Available from LifeWay Christian Resources Customer Service; One LifeWay Plaza; Nashville, TN 37234-0113; by fax at (615)251-5993; by calling toll-free 1-800-458-2772; by e-mail at *orderentry@lifeway.com;* by ordering online at *www.lifeway.com;* or by visiting the LifeWay Christian Store serving you.

3. J. I. Packer. *Knowing God* (Downer's Grove, IL: InterVarsity Press, 1973), 221-229.

4. Os Guinness. *The Call* (Nashville: Word Publishing, 1998), 4.

week two

SHOWING
WE CARE

"He who walks with the wise
grows wise, but a companion of fools
suffers harm." *Proverbs 13:20*

"I'm confused," Sarah confided to her group leader. "I really want to help women in our Bible study because so many of them are struggling with life. Francis has a chronically sick child, Jane's alcoholic husband can't keep a job, Jackie's mother died a few weeks ago, and Ruth learned yesterday that she has breast cancer. When I signed up for the Bible study, I didn't know there were so many hurting people in our church."

Sarah's predicament is common for those who genuinely care for troubled people. Sarah's compassion propels her to want to help, but she needs to define her goals of helping so she won't become a casualty herself. God has made people as relational beings. We are deeply wounded in relationships, yet relationships are the means by which we can experience forgiveness and healing. We most powerfully and fully absorb truth if it's modeled and taught by a trusted friend who cares deeply about our woundedness.

Out of her compassion, Sarah was willing to initiate contact. Often, people come to us instead of our seeking them because they desperately need a friend. Their problems might be acute or chronic, financial or relational, about themselves or about someone they love. All they know is that they can't figure things out on their own. At this critical moment we can walk with them to impart wisdom, hope, and support.

THE ROLE OF YOUR PASTOR

Most pastors recognize that their role is not to become professional counselors to provide long-term, intensive care for people in their churches and communities. Most of them haven't been trained to be professional therapists, and their duties to shepherd God's flock require their time and attention in reaching the lost, discipling new believers, and developing leaders.

For this reason, many of them use a short-term model of counseling that provides immediate and compassionate care but recognizes the limitations of their role. The model we recommend for *A Trusted Friend When It Matters Most* is the one many pastors use.

Always make sure that you are not duplicating or interfering with the pastor's counsel to individuals, couples, and families. You certainly don't want to be critical of him or his advice. The pastor is ultimately responsible for all areas of church life. Be submissive to his leadership and his vision for a trusted friends' ministry.

A SHORT-TERM MODEL

This model consists of three or four meetings (some of which can be a phone call, an e-mail, or a note in the mail). Then refer them to a counselor, agency, or organization that can provide long-term, intensive help. These meetings are:

- First, gathering basic information, hearing the first explanation of the problem, and observing the person's condition
- Second, attempting to determine the actual problem, and more often, beginning to uncover the web of complex issues in the lives of most hurting people
- Third, if necessary, bringing in other family members to become a part of the discovery and healing process
- Fourth, making a referral, explaining the benefits of the counselor or agency or organization, and outlining the steps to connect with the resource

What might be some benefits and liabilities of a short-term instead of a long-term approach for a trusted friend?

Benefits

Liabilities

Generally, pastors and trusted friends follow up in a month to six weeks to ensure that the individual or family has connected with a helping person or organization. There are, of course, many different models of counseling and almost as many models in Christian counseling. Genuinely Christ-centered care, though, contains some common, important elements. It acknowledges:
- the legitimate expression of emotions in the process of uncovering hidden perceptions and wounds and in the resolution and healing of those wounds
- that many of the problems people experience result from attempts to meet genuine needs in ways apart from God's design
- that Christ-centered counseling can only be provided by a person whose faith in Christ provides empathy, love, insight, and direction
- that the truth of Scripture is the first and foremost source of wisdom and insight about the human condition, needs, and remedies

- the need to carefully observe each person's situation to see how the Scriptures can be applied most specifically and powerfully
- the importance of a powerful blend of God's work and our responsibility, of the Holy Spirit's power and the role of spiritual disciplines

As you serve in the role of a trusted friend, realize that your care for people is in the tradition of countless others who trusted Christ to use them in tender and powerful ways to transform the lives of hurting, needy people.

PREVIEWING THE PROCESS

Anthony and Daniel had been friends since college. They were both amazed to find that they now lived in the same city, although 30 minutes away from each other. They got reacquainted at a motivational training event and had kept in touch since then. Daniel was pleased to hear that Anthony and Gina would have their first child soon.

The night of Melissa's birth, Daniel was there with a balloon and a card waiting for Anthony to tell him he could come see the baby. Instead, Anthony came to the waiting room and collapsed into the nearest chair. He buried his face in his hands and began weeping.

"Is Melissa OK? Is Gina OK?" Daniel asked.

"Melissa has Down syndrome."

Daniel waited for what seemed an eternity. Finally, Anthony spoke. "I don't know what to do. I can't fix this. Daniel, help me know what to do."

This type of story is repeated every minute of every day. Someone needs help, and we simply don't know what to do.

As we explore the short-term model of care, don't worry if you feel inadequate to follow these steps. Training in how to accomplish this process will follow. For now just give each step and its questions your best guess. If you don't know an answer, skip it.

The goal for being a trusted friend is not to resolve years of problems but to be a step—a crucial step, but only a step—in God's plan to restore a person, a couple, and perhaps a family to wholeness in Christ. To accomplish this goal, a trusted friend will:

- Connect with the person by showing empathy and support.

What are some practical ways to connect with people so they feel safe to be honest with you?

- Identify the problem, or at least begin to uncover the real problem often buried under years of excusing, rationalizing, and denying.

  What are some signs you could look for?

  What are some questions you might ask?

- Instill a strong sense of hope that God provides forgiveness for every sin, strength to endure every difficulty, and wisdom to find His path and follow it.

  What passages of Scripture have provided comfort and encouragement when you were hurting?

- Begin to educate hurting people about the issues they face such as grief, manipulation, trust, forgiveness, and taking responsibility.

  Can you think of a book, movie, television documentary, or other source that comes to mind that has made an incredible impression on your life?

- Find the best resources to meet needs, including each aspect of their lives: relational, spiritual, physical, and financial.

  Name some Christian counselors or godly adults you already trust.

What are some resources you'd recommend for those in debt?

or chronically or critically ill?

or with children who are out of control?

• Assist people in taking the next step to connect with the resources they need.

How can you refer people to a professional resource while still communicating that you have not dropped them as a friend?

• Stay in touch occasionally to offer support and insight about the process of change and growth.

What are some ways you can tell if the person appreciates your continued involvement?

or if you've become a nuisance?

This model of care may require some major adjustments if we feel led by God to pursue being a trusted friend. We are compassionate people who are eager and willing to do anything to help people in need. This compassion is certainly a wonderful, God-given strength, but our zeal to help runs the risk of jumping into the deep end of the pool where we can't swim!

We may find problems we never dreamed existed, such as bipolar disorder, personality disorders, financial fraud, sexual addictions, and a host of other complicated and difficult issues in people's lives. If we have offered ourselves as a permanent and complete resource for the hurting person (and we don't have to use those exact words to communicate that we see ourselves as the one, final, and only thing the hurting person needs), we will eventually disappoint the people we want to help and burn out personally because we can't bear the load.

God has given each of us strengths and experiences that equip us to care for hurting people, and it's important for us to identify those strengths. You may react with boldness or caution in relationships; appreciate the way God has made you and yet make some adjustments when they are necessary.

week two

If you use this short-term model, would you have to make adjustments to your usual way of relating to individuals, couples, and families?   ❏ yes   ❏ no   ❏ not sure

What is a danger of long-term involvement in other people's problems?

The model that we're using in this resource clarifies our goals, provides a guide for interactions, and quickly gets people to the professional help or other resources they often need. Become skilled in this model and use it to prevent yourself from getting drawn too deeply into people's problems.

CARE IN TIMES OF CRISIS

Crises may occur in an instant without warning, or they may have given signals that were disregarded for years. All of us dread the thought of a knock on our door with a police officer waiting to give us the awful news, but others have stuck their proverbial heads in the sand year after year to avoid the painful reality of a strained marriage, a broken relationship with a parent or child, or a serious health problem.

35

One day the truth crashes in, and people suffer the trauma of a suicide attempt, panic attack, or terminal disease. For most people the shock of this news puts them in the first stage of grief. They will need your help in the coming days, weeks, and months. In times of crises, our role as trusted friends consists of four steps:

1. Make a connection: Some people instantly reach out for help when they experience trauma; others withdraw into an emotional shell. The first step, then, is to make contact with people to assure them that they aren't alone.

2. First decisions: Quite often people who have experienced trauma are in shock. They have difficulty thinking clearly, and they can't focus on the immediate needs and decisions. In many cases, giving directions isn't enough. Take the person with you to the morgue, hospital, funeral home, or wherever the need is. Offer to call family and friends to tell them the news. Ask a pastor to come to comfort and pray. Secure food and anything else necessary for the person to make it through those first terrible hours and days. Your goal in the early hours of the crisis is to provide comfort and reduce anxiety. "Just showing up" will help the traumatized person. During the hours of shock, you may need to make decisions or at least offer your suggestions about the best course to take regarding a host of important and immediate decisions.

3. Get help: Even days later traumatic events can leave people in a sustained state of shock. Offer to contact a doctor, pastor, attorney, or family members, and recruit additional people to help shoulder the burden of care. Give the person lots of space to weep and laugh at memories of happier times. Practical help means a great deal to those in crisis: cleaning the house to prepare for out-of town guests, mowing the lawn, grocery shopping, answering the phone or door bell, preparing thank-you notes, or walking the dog. If out-of-town travel is necessary, arrange to have the mail and newspaper delivery suspended. Suggest that someone house-sit or at least care for plants and pets.

4. Adjustments: An observant, though somewhat cynical, man once said, "Church people will care for you for two weeks. After that, you're on your own." In too many situations his observation is accurate. In many churches people rush to the aid of someone who has experienced a crisis, but after a week or two, the calls

stop coming and the casserole dishes have all been returned. The grieving person then feels terribly alone. Part of being a friend to people in crisis is to realize that these people have just begun the grieving process. They have a long, long way to go! Two weeks later, six months later, and two years later, they still need a friend who will provide a shoulder to cry on, a laugh to lighten their day, and insights about the goodness of God.

Think of someone who recently experienced a traumatic event.
Write a plan for how you would have tried to care for that person:

in the first hours:

in the first few days:

in the first few months:

We live in a fallen world, and crises are a too common occurrence. Whether they come from accidents, disease, hurricanes, tornadoes, or broken relationships, traumas leave people in shock and require their friends to come to their side to provide assistance. People in the throes of crisis may not have the presence of mind to thank you (or even acknowledge you) as you help, but realize that you are extending the hands and heart of God at a vulnerable moment in their lives.

CARE AS DISCIPLESHIP

A young woman called a church on Sunday morning. In an agitated voice she said, "Hello. My name is Melody. I'm … I need to talk to somebody as soon as possible. I'm having a panic attack and I don't know what to do." The person answering Melody's call told her, "Sorry, everybody's in Sunday School. Could you call back tomorrow?"

Needless to say, she never called them back. Melody did, however, find another church where she not only got help with her panic attacks but also trusted the Lord, was baptized, and became an active leader of the young singles class. Carol, the pastor's wife, was privileged to disciple Melody, keeping her supplied with devotional and other Christian literature and meeting with her often.

Our time with those in need is not an addition to discipleship; it is discipleship. We intersect their lives at a point of need, perhaps when they are more open to God, biblical insight, and repentance than any other time in their lives. God has given us the privilege of stepping into that moment to represent Him and to provide encouragement as people grope for answers to life's biggest questions.

Today many Christians expect the Christian life to be a helicopter ride to the top of the mountain—a relatively effortless and pain-free experience—and they are deeply disappointed when it is not. Instead, the Christian life is much more like a hike in the mountains, full of determination and grit, with encouraging companions, hard-won battles, and beautiful views along the way.

For those who prefer the illusion of a helicopter ride, they shape their expectations of God with a powerful combination of perfectionism, instant gratification, and victimization. These factors create the expectation that God's primary goal is to make them happy (instead of deepening their dependence on Him) and to fix their problems (instead of using their problems to shape their lives). They remain passive and stagnant (instead of taking responsibility for their growth and change). How they perceive God's will must be addressed by someone who steps into their lives with strength, love, and truth.

Our purpose is to help these people trust God so that they are transformed by His love, power, and forgiveness. But make no mistake: This is hard work! As Paul wrote to the Colossians, "We proclaim [Christ], admonishing and teaching everyone with all wisdom, so that we may present everyone perfect in Christ. To this end I labor, struggling with all his energy, which so powerfully works in me" (Col. 1:28-29).

> Paul's language about his role in discipleship sounds like a lot of work! Does his description (a) stimulate you or (b) discourage you? (underline)

Whatever their cause, painful experiences can be stepping stones of spiritual growth—if, and only if, people turn to God to gain a deeper grasp of His heart and His purposes. We naturally try to avoid trouble at all costs, but living in a fallen world with a fallen nature necessarily means we will experience difficulties.

Paul recognized that times of trouble are hothouses of spiritual growth. His perspective was "Bring it on!" He wrote to the believers in Rome: "We also rejoice in our sufferings, because we know that suffering produces perseverance; perseverance, character; and character, hope. And hope does not disappoint us, because God has poured out his love into our hearts by the Holy Spirit, whom he has given us" (Rom. 5:3-5).

The production of perseverance, godly character, and genuine hope in God in times of trouble doesn't happen instantly. God uses the powerful blend of His Word, His Spirit's power, and the loving, honest support of His people to help others take step after step to walk with Him in grace and truth. Like the development of an oak tree, spiritual growth requires nourishment, light, and time. If any of these is lacking, the sapling—and even a mature tree—withers and dies. Our role as trusted friends is to supply these requirements, or at least to point people to resources where they can experience them.

Compare the needs of a growing tree to the needs of someone experiencing emotional healing and spiritual growth.

nourishment

light

time

Some Christians, and especially wounded ones, fail to comprehend the blend of God's work plus our responsibility to respond in faith. In desperation, they may say, "I need to just let go and let God. I need to get out of the way and let Him do His thing in my life." That comment has some validity in terms of choosing God's ways over our selfish ways, but it can confuse young or hurting people about the nature of spiritual life.

We need to understand the interplay of God's part and our part. Many passages describe our total abandonment to God, and many other passages instruct us to obey God's directives. How do we put those together? Are they mutually exclusive?

One of the clearest and strongest descriptions of the blend of our responsibility and God's work is in Paul's Letter to the Philippians. After his beautiful and powerful depiction of the humility and glory of Christ, he instructed the believers, "Therefore … continue to work out your salvation with fear and trembling, for it is God who works in you to will and to act according to his good purpose" (Phil. 2:12-13). Do healing and growth come from God's work or our efforts? Paul said clearly it's a powerful blend of both.

People will be confused and disappointed if they simply sit back and wait for God to fix them and make their pain go away. Spiritual growth and emotional healing is much more like rehab for a broken leg. We put ourselves in the care of a physician or therapist who knows what's best for us, but we have to do the work of exercise, eating right, and resting to strengthen the leg. In the same way, we trust God to work in our lives to give us wisdom and direction, but we also play a vital role as we follow His directions to drink in the nourishment of truth and exercise faith in God's sovereignty and goodness.

What is the patient's part in rehab initiating from a broken leg?

What is the physical therapist's part?

What makes the patient want to quit?

What motivates the patient to keep going no matter what it takes?

COMMON MISCONCEPTIONS

Kim was in a women's Bible study with Candace. After class one day, Kim noticed that Candace looked discouraged, and in fact, she had seemed to be having a hard time concentrating. Kim approached her and asked, "Candace, is there something going on? You seem kind of down today."

Candace asked if they could find a place to talk privately. There, after only a moment of hesitation, a torrent of words began to flow. She explained that her husband was harsh and mean to her and her two young sons, but then her expression changed. She spoke in a voice full of sadness and tinged with guilt, "I guess I'm just a bad wife. I guess I deserve the husband I've got."

Over the next several weeks Kim met with Candace several times to talk. In these conversations more of her story unfolded: a lifetime of feeling unloved, more details of a troubled marriage, crushing debt, children out of control, and emotional numbness from feeling overwhelmed by it all. Kim helped her find a Christian counselor. Though her husband wouldn't go to the counselor with her, Candace found for the first time in her life that she could be strong and trust God through even her darkest times.

As months went by Kim and Candace continued to see one another in the Bible study class and at occasional lunches together. During those months Candace's life changed. Kim's friendship had been the catalyst for hope for her and her sons.

When Kim thinks about Candace, she smiles. *I'm so thrilled that God would use me to help her. Nothing gives me more pleasure!*

Kim's story is echoed by countless men and women, young and old, who noticed a need in someone's life and took a step or two to meet that need.

Can you see yourself as a "Kim" to someone else?
❑ yes ❑ maybe ❑ no

What would be the hardest part for you? (circle)

time   compassion   finding resources   initiating   confidence

What part of helping people would give you the most pleasure?

Victims of trauma, abuse, or abandonment; addicts, and many others who experience emotional damage believe that their lives are "normal" and "will always be this way." One of our main goals, then, is to help them gain a new grasp of reality. Here are some common misconceptions and corrections:

1. "What happened to me is what I deserved." This sense of despair is most common with those who experienced abuse or abandonment in their early years. They need someone to hear their story and to give honest feedback: "What you experienced is terrible. I'm so sorry that happened to you." This gives them permission to enter the healing process.

2. Many victims internalize their pain and anger. They often feel intense shame, self-hatred, and depression. Your love and your communication of their new identity in Christ will help them gain a new sense of strength (Eph. 1:3-14: loved, chosen, adopted, forgiven, sealed; 1 Pet. 2:9-10).

3. For many who suffer prolonged, painful times in their lives, shame is lived out on a daily basis with oppressive guilt feelings and thoughts. Victims feel they can never measure up, they can't do enough to compensate for past sins (real or imagined), and they will never find peace and joy. Address this guilt with the gospel message of God's incredible love and forgiveness for all those who are guilty and need God's forgiveness (Peter after his betrayal, Paul after capturing and killing believers, the thief on the cross, etc.).

4. Hurt necessarily fuels anger at the offender, but often this anger is repressed and internalized into depression. Look for the many faces of anger (sometimes rage, sometimes compulsive busyness, sometimes numbness, sometimes pseudo-sweetness, etc.). Most wounded people feel tremendously guilty for being angry, especially at those who hurt them. They need to understand that the feeling of anger isn't wrong (see Eph. 4:26), but revengeful expressions of anger are wrong (see Jas. 1:20). They also need to learn to use their anger as a window into their hearts to see the hurt, grieve the wounds, forgive the offender, and learn to set new boundaries in relationships. (That's a lot different than the message "You shouldn't feel angry!")

5. Most people don't know how to grieve, but it's a learned skill that is absolutely necessary for emotional and spiritual healing. The psalms of lament give us a wonderful example of honesty, disappointment, and new hope that comes from the grieving process. But that process takes time and attention. It doesn't just happen, and it can't be rushed. The first step of overcoming denial by uncovering

the depths of a person's wound may take weeks or months. Then the stages of grief can be processed over many months or years.

6. It is normal and necessary for hurting people to develop patterns of self-protection, but these protections also have some negative consequences. Three of the most common forms of self-protection include wanting to (1) please others at all cost, (2) prove yourself by perfectionism or achievement, or (3) hide from any risk of conflict. In discipleship these patterns can be addressed in several ways. They may be normal and reasonable in an abusive situation, but they can become barriers to relationships with God and other people. We can help these people by uncovering the causes of this behavior and addressing the fear that fuels it. People won't give up their self-protective behavior, however, until and unless they are convinced they feel safe with their trusted friend. That level of trust takes time and must be proven.

7. One of the most difficult issues of the victim-mentality is the consuming demand for justice, compensation, and guarantees. Victims were acted upon by the person who inflicted the pain, and they remain passive, demanding that others fix their problems. They demand that the ones who hurt them pay for their wrongs (which might look more like revenge than justice). They demand that someone (spouse, friends, children, and now, perhaps you) fill up the hole created by the one who hurt them, and they demand that no one ever hurt them again—which, of course, is quite unrealistic. The victim-mentality is corrected by focusing on the underlying hurts and fears, as well as addressing the actual behaviors of anger, passivity, controlling people by self-pity, and manipulation of others.

8. Victims, by definition, have had their boundaries stomped on. Most of them live with such shame and confusion that they don't even know what decisions they can make for themselves. Learning to set boundaries is a function of a new perspective, a new identity, courage, and wisdom.

9. Ultimately a wounded person needs the same things others need (love, modeling, encouragement, application of Scripture) but applied to a deeper level and with more patience on the part of the trusted friend. This blend of truth, grace, and time is essential in establishing reasonable expectations for you and the wounded widow.

Which of the principles of discipling wounded people have you personally experienced? Circle the number beside each of them.

Which of these are ongoing situations for you? Put a star beside each one.

What are some ways you can get the help you need?

EIGHT KEYS TO HELPING WOUNDED PEOPLE

To point people to Christ and help them grow in their faith, consider these suggestions:

1. Learn to apply the Scriptures more deeply in your own life and in your role as a trusted friend. Use illustrations about shame and identity, guilt and forgiveness, bitterness and repentance, and all the other topics we've looked at. Show how the gospel message (which is the heart of growing in Christ too) meets our deepest needs.

2. Be aware of symptoms of abuse, depression, grief, and other signs of woundedness in those you meet, especially the self-protective behaviors of pleasing, proving, and hiding. Learn to ask probing but appropriate questions. If people open up, then use that opportunity to teach the person about the patterns of behavior and the emotional damage that comes from being a victim of abuse or abandonment.

3. Demystify the person's perceptions. Many hurting people believe they are alone, and to be honest, they think they are crazy. One of the most important things they can learn is that their feelings and behaviors are totally reasonable as a response to abuse or abandonment.

4. When hurting people realize their thoughts, feelings, and behaviors are normal for someone who has endured their pain, they will be more likely to talk openly about what happened. Don't push this, and don't fear this. Give permission to be honest, listen carefully, and don't give simplistic answers. Your presence means far more than a theological cliché.

5. Look for opportunities to communicate the message of redemption. People have come because they recognize their need. At first they may not have framed their need as a spiritual one, but as you've talked with them, they may realize that their hurts are a reflection of their need for Christ's forgiveness. Sensitively and lovingly share the message of the gospel, and assure them of God's great love. You may see more people come to Christ through this ministry than any other in the church.

6. Help people practice spiritual disciplines. God's part is to change lives. Our part is to do things that will fill our minds with good and godly thoughts so the Holy Spirit has something to work with! Spiritual disciples are time-tested practices to fill our minds with truth and focus our hearts on Christ. In some cases, hurting people are already involved in reflection, confession, prayer, journaling, Bible study, connecting with other believers, worship, service, and giving. They simply need to go to a deeper level in grasping and applying insights from God's Word. But many of the hurting people we encounter have never developed these habits of the faith, and they need you to teach and model them. As these behaviors become habits, people will learn to gain more from God on their own.

7. Provide available resources. Does the government offer any mental health services? Are there books they can get? Groups they can attend? Counselors they can see? Even if no official services are available, your love and your application of Scripture to their level of pain will provide wonderful help to them. Books can help people gain insights, but literature is only part of the solution. Hurting people need to see and feel love from a trusted friend, and they need encouragement to take steps of faith to carve out a new way to live.

8. Don't focus on their pain all the time. Dealing with wounds can be all consuming— for the victim and the caregiver. Carve out time to do fun things together. Help them laugh, spend time with others, and find joy in life.

Pick two of the keys and write an action you can do to help others acquire those skills in becoming a trusted friend.

1.

2.

GOD'S CALL

Becoming a trusted friend is a solemn responsibility. This week we wanted to give you a sense of context so you can see how your role is an extension of God's call for the church to reach the lost and disciple believers, including those who are suffering, discouraged, broken, or alone.

We cannot impart what we don't possess, so as this week's content ends, take some time to reflect on the ways God has healed your heart when it was broken, times He restored your sense of hope, and the people He used to impart grace and truth to you.

If you've learned to trust God through suffering, you've learned to persevere. God has shaped your character, and you found more hope than ever before. You've become wise. Those who walk with you will become wise, also. That's the goal and joy of being a trusted friend.

The Stages of Grief are in the Appendix on page 122. We'll discuss the first three during your group session. You may read them now or after group time. Your group leader will go over all of the material in the appendices during your study.

What key idea or understanding have you learned this week?

What steps will you take to make what you've learned a part of your life and your care for others?

BECOMING A GREAT LISTENER

"My dear brothers, take note of this: Everyone should be quick to listen, slow to speak and slow to become angry."
James 1:19

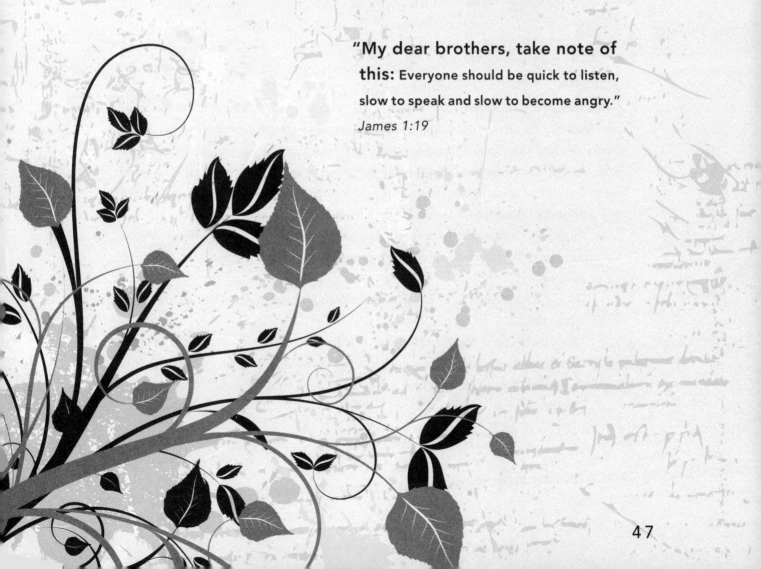

When my (Pat's) children were little, I often came home late in the afternoon, spent some time with them, and then sat down to watch the news. One day that schedule didn't suit little Catherine. As I turned my attention to the news anchor, she wanted me to stay focused on her. She kept talking, and I tried to listen to Catherine and television at the same time. That didn't work. She knew she wasn't connecting with me, so she came over to my chair and crawled up in my lap. She put her hands on my cheeks and turned my face from the television toward her, and then she told me, "Dad, I'm over here!"

The first task of a trusted friend is to listen well so that people feel understood. It's not enough for us to understand the facts they are telling us. They need to be convinced that we're connected to their hearts as well as to their circumstances. This week we'll examine the steps to becoming an even better listener.

Reflect on your experiences in conversations—both positive and negative—and jot down two or three words that describe a good listener.

LONGING TO FEEL HEARD

Sarah had gone to a women's Bible study for a couple of years. Although she was quiet and reserved, she joined in the discussions each week. One week the leader of the group, Becky, noticed that Sarah seemed stressed. The signs may not have been noticeable to anyone else, but Becky made a point of observing people in her group so she could address their real needs, spoken or unspoken. After the study that week, as Sarah walked toward the door Becky called to her, "Sarah, do you have just a minute?"

"Sure," Sarah responded as she turned around. She looked startled by Becky's simple question. She walked back to the now empty table and asked, "What is it? Did I say something wrong?"

"No," Becky assured her." I was just wondering. Are you OK? You seemed a bit preoccupied today."

"No. No, I'm fine," Sarah tried to convince her.

"If you need anything—like somebody to talk to—I'd be glad to talk with you anytime." Becky then asked, "You have my number, don't you?"

"Yes, but I'm fine. I really am."

Becky smiled, "Good. I'll see you next week."

But the next week Sarah looked even more stressed. She had a hard time following the discussion, and she seemed frustrated when she couldn't find a passage of Scripture as quickly as the other ladies. After the study Becky made a point of putting her arm around Sarah and giving her a hug. No words—just a big, warm hug. Sarah looked surprised, but she smiled and thanked Becky.

For several weeks, Becky could tell that Sarah was going through a difficult time, but Sarah deflected Becky's questions and expressions of love. Finally, Becky asked her, "Can we get together tomorrow to talk?"

Reluctantly, Sarah agreed, and in the conversation the next day, she poured out her heartache of finding marijuana in her son's dresser drawer as she was putting away laundry. He said it wasn't his and to stay out of his room.

"I wish you had told me about this a couple of months ago," Becky gently told her as she put her hand on Sarah's arm to comfort her.

Sarah began sobbing. Through her tears, she told Becky, "I just couldn't. I was afraid the other women in the group would condemn me … or call a police officer … or gossip about me. And I just couldn't take that."

Becky's perceptive and persistent kindness broke down the barrier that prevented Sarah from being honest about her pain. Sarah's trust in Becky grew over the next few conversations. Becky directed her to a Christian counselor in their area who specialized in adolescent issues. The two ladies became close friends who shared hurts and joys with each other for many years. Sarah also felt accepted by the group.

When people feel understood, some wonderful things happen:

- Barriers to the person's progress are identified so resources can be marshaled to meet needs.
- Loneliness and shame melt away in the warmth of trust.
- A sense of hope begins to flicker and then flame in the person's heart.

Was there a time when you confided in a friend and you felt understood? If so, what were some of the feelings you experienced? (circle)

relief   embarrassment   hope   fear   joy

Other _____

Has there ever been a time when you tried to share a need with someone and you didn't feel understood? If so, on a scale of awful to good, how did that experience affect:

	AWFUL	GOOD
your mood		
your relationship		
your confidence		

COMPLEXITIES OF COMMUNICATION

Many of us have played a game in which a person whispers in another's ear and the message is passed around the room. By the time it gets back to the first person, the message is usually much different—and often hilariously different!

Communication between two people is notoriously complicated. At least four variables fight against clarity and understanding:

- What I said
- What I thought I said
- What you heard
- What you thought you heard

Good listening skills sort out complexities and eliminate some of the misunderstandings that can easily occur when two people try to communicate with each other. These essential skills should be practiced at home, at work, with friends, and with neighbors. Some of us are more naturally gifted than others in being good listeners, but all of us—even tired dads who want to relax and watch the news—can learn and practice these skills.

LISTENING SKILLS

We'll address these listening skills:

- Initiating
- Attending
- Active listening
- Responding
- Referring

INITIATING

Needs come in all shapes and sizes, and they wear many faces. The death of a child devastates a couple. Debt can consume a family. A natural disaster can destroy a home and leave people with only the clothes on their backs. A person struggling with a dead-end job may need direction and advice. An addict may need to find a facility to detoxify and begin recovery, and the addict's family members need to find truth in the midst of all the lies and deception common in these situations. No matter what the circumstances, trusted friends notice and initiate assistance or respond to the person's request with a warm smile and a simple question, "How can I help you?"

Rob had been in the Men's Ministry small group for several months. He had been an eager participant in the discussions. A few weeks ago Dwayne noticed that Rob's demeanor changed. He hardly said a word. Dwayne directed questions to him, but he gave only quick, superficial answers. Last week, when the other men gave input to the discussion, Rob made a point of disagreeing with them. He seemed angry … really angry. Out of the corner of his eye Dwayne saw some of the men looking at each other as if to say, *What's going on with this guy?* As the meeting ended, Dwayne found a moment alone with Rob and said, "You've seemed a little tense today. If something is bothering you, I'd be glad to talk to you about it."

Some people are independent and have never had to ask for help, and some have experienced trauma so severe that their hearts are numb and their minds are blank. Your question, and the implied offer to help, opens the door to information and trust, two vital ingredients in your role as a trusted friend.

Read John 5:1-9. How did Jesus initiate conversation with the crippled man? Circle your answer.

statement   question

What response did the man give?

❏ No, thanks.
❏ Someone else is going to take care of it.
❏ I like my life just as it is.
❏ People have been taking advantage of me.

Put a star next to the response(s) you most often give when someone offers help.

ATTENDING

My (Pat's) pastor is one of the world's best in attending as he listens. Whenever he's talking with someone—in the church foyer after the service, in the hallway, in his office during the week, at McDonald's™ (his favorite place to study), or anywhere else—Rick is fully present. He looks the person in the eyes and gives his complete attention. Nothing—a crowd of people waiting to talk to him, the ceiling collapsing, or his busy lifestyle—distracts him.

Attending involves several important elements:

Make eye contact: If people aren't making eye contact with me when I'm talking with them, I assume they aren't really listening and maybe they don't really care. In the same way, if I'm genuinely tracking with someone, I look intently to gauge the person's mood and the connection between words and expressions. We'll explore more about eye contact on page 53, "Active Listening."

Do you find it easy to make eye contact?

❑ no   ❑ sometimes   ❑ usually

How do you feel when someone doesn't make eye contact with you?

_____

How do you feel when they do? _____

_____

Which is easier? ❑ make eye contact ❑ keep eye contact

Avoid distractions: In our world a thousand sights and sounds call for our attention, but we need to cut through all those and rivet our attention on the person in front of us. If we can't concentrate in a loud or busy environment, we can say, "I'm having a hard time paying attention with all the things going on around here. Can we move over to that table (or go to a different location or find another time to meet)?"

What does it tell you when you are talking to someone who leaves on a television program, a loud CD player, or a radio?

❏ not interested
❏ thinks he or she can do two things at one time
❏ feels insecure
❏ wants to connect with you

Look interested: Even if you're completely tracking with the person's every word, you'll lose him or her if you don't convey that you're interested in what he or she has to say. Facial expressions, gestures, posture, and verbal feedback assure the person that you really are listening and do care about them.

Fatigue and boredom can cripple our attempts to attend to people. When we're tired, our minds tend to wander, we slump in our seats, and we yawn. That's not the way to communicate compassion! And some people talk on and on and on about the same tired subject. At those times, we want to scream! But we need to remember that people who talk too much often are problem-solving as they tell the story once more. Listen for the real message beneath the torrent of words. Actually they are telling you how much they long to be heard.

When you're tired or bored, make a special effort to sit up, look the person in the eye, and give a little more feedback than usual. That will help you stay focused on the person's words and needs. Also, it might help to write notes as the person talks. Many people feel honored that you care enough to write down what is being said.

Find a mirror and imagine you look each of these ways.

interested and engaged   distracted   bored   tired

The next time you listen to someone, practice looking interested, leaning forward, and making eye contact.

ACTIVE LISTENING

After initiating the conversation by asking, "How can I help you?" and giving your full attention to the person, you become a type of detective to discover the real needs and the complicating factors in the person's life. To be a good detective:

Ask clarifying questions: As people tell their stories about strained or broken relationships, death or disease, or needs of any type, ask questions such as: "What happened next?" or "How did you feel when that happened?" If the description of the situation or relationship seems important and you want to know more, don't ask "why" questions. Instead, invite the person to elaborate—"Tell me more about that." Quite often "why" questions ("Why did you do that?" "Why did you say that to her?") imply the person was wrong, and it puts people on the defensive. The "why" question can shut down a conversation at the moment people begin to share their deepest hurts and needs.

Read nonverbal signals: Look for consistency in the person's nonverbal signals to see if the words and actions are the same. For instance, a lady with a dejected expression can tell you that she's fine, but her face and posture speaks far more loudly and articulately than her words. Look for clues in how the person dresses, talks about friends or work, and doesn't look at you directly. Other signals might help you look beneath the surface.

> Think of an important conversation you've had in the last few days. What were some visual clues you picked up on (or you wish you had picked up on)?

Wait during silence: Some of us feel uncomfortable with silence during conversations, so we fill in the holes with advice, directions, and personal stories. Avoid that temptation. Instead, if you've asked a question and you're sure the person understands, wait for an answer. The person may be wrestling with some of the most important issues in life. It takes time to get a grip on those to articulate them!

> What is your normal response when people are silent for a while?
>
> ❏ I'm silent too.
> ❏ I want to fill up the blank space.
> ❏ I say, "You probably feel like this," and give an example.
> ❏ I'm afraid I went too far with my questions. I get nervous and fidget.

When you encounter silence, consider that the longer the silence, the more important the issue. If the person still doesn't respond after several minutes, ask, "Can I help you find a handle for your thoughts? If you'd like, you can begin talking, and we'll sort it out together." Don't push. If the person isn't ready, your kindness and patience may provide the safety for a deeper conversation next time.

> In your next group meeting be prepared to explain how silence can be an important part of a rich, meaningful conversation.

Summarize the content: After the person has explained an important topic, provide a summary as feedback and clarification. You can say, "This is what I hear you saying," and then explain the situation in your own words. Many times people respond with relief that somebody finally understands, but quite often they correct a misunderstanding or two to make sure you get an accurate picture. That builds trust.

Mirror feelings: Both facts and feelings are important parts of people's stories. God made us with emotions, and as trusted friends, we need to value the feelings of those we help. One of the most effective techniques in surfacing and validating emotions is "mirroring." We make simple, declarative statements about the feelings we see and hear in the person, such as, "That hurt," "You enjoyed that," or "You felt very sad and alone."

Avoid the temptation to make these statements into questions by adding, "didn't you?" Adding the question invites only a yes or no answer, but a declarative statement elicits a richer, deeper response, such as, "Yes, I felt hurt and alone. In fact, I've never felt so alone in my life." This kind of interaction often opens the floodgates of long repressed feelings. Don't be shocked by them, and don't be afraid of them. Tears, fear, and anger are part of the healing process. People honor us when they trust us with their deepest hurts and highest hopes.

> Mirroring affirms people's emotions and invites them to take the next step in emotional vulnerability. Write an example of mirroring.
>
> He said: "I hate my job. It's a dead end. I work hard, but no one cares."
>
> You say:

She said: "I'm not sure what to do about my marriage. Our love seems to have grown cold."

You say:

Avoid giving answers too quickly: Some of us are fixers. When we find a problem, we're quick to fix it. In the discovery phase of being a trusted friend, don't rush to provide solutions. There will be time for that, but for now focus your attention on digging down through the layers of confusion, denial, and numbness to uncover reality in the person's life. When problems are accurately identified, solutions present themselves far more easily. But when we jump to conclusions and try to fix only the surface problems, we become obstacles to insight, understanding, trust, and genuine steps forward.

How does it feel to you when someone gives you a quick answer?

unheard   accepted   disappointed   surprised   devalued   curious

Is giving a quick answer (or seeking to solve the problem) characteristic of you? ❏ yes ❏ no

Avoid judging and condemning: People can tell if love is authentic, and they can surely tell if we condemn them. If we are judgmental, we may be smiling on the outside, but inside we want to blast them with truth so they will repent! Love, though, covers a multitude of sins—theirs and ours.

Jesus didn't condemn the tax collectors who betrayed their countrymen, the woman caught in adultery, lepers, outcasts, or anyone else who suffered or wandered off God's chosen course for their lives. He extended grace and truth, not one or the other. Most people won't listen to truth unless they are first convinced that we love them. That's the model of Jesus' ministry, and that's the model for trusted friends.

Read John 8:1-11. Imagine being that woman. In your group talk about how you would have felt when the religious leaders grabbed you. How would you have felt when Jesus treated you kindly?

Practice immediacy: Some of the people we help are lost in a world of conflicting thoughts and emotions. They have tried to make sense of years of abuse, abandonment, heartache, bitterness, depression, addictions, lies, and a host of other difficulties in their own lives and their most important relationships. They need help to sort these things out. These people have lived with tremendous stress most of their lives, and it has become "normalized." They don't even realize they feel stress any more. They have difficulty being objective. As a person tells you about a difficult situation or painful moment, the person's words and emotions may not match up. Stop the conversation and ask, "Tell me, what's going on in your heart right now?" or "Let me stop you for just a minute. As you describe the situation, what are you feeling?"

What are some reasons people may not connect their emotions with the painful situations they describe when you listen to them?

What reactions would you expect if you ask them how they are feeling?

In the past, the person has thought about that event a million times, but the pain was so intense that he became disconnected from it at some point. By practicing immediacy, you will help the person connect the event with the emotion again. This moment and this realization can be quite painful, but it's the path to honesty, emotional integrity, grief, and healing. This technique is also useful as you mediate (serve as a go-between) in conversations with spouses, parents and children, or any others.

RESPONDING

So far in the process of listening you have been uncovering facts and clarifying events and emotions. Of course, you have been responding by asking questions and providing affirmation that you understand. But when you sense that you have a good grasp of the problem, you can respond more fully with comfort, encouragement, information, and perhaps correction.

The short-term model of care includes two conversations that focus on discovery, so don't rush to give answers. It's far better to ask a few extra questions and prolong the discovery phase than to come to incorrect conclusions too quickly.

One of the biggest problems many of us face in this ministry is the false assumption that other people are just like us and will respond to problems just like we do. When someone tells us about a problem in her marriage, we need to avoid any temptation to instantly assume her problems are the same as any we've faced. They may be similar, but they may be quite different. Certainly our experiences shape our lives and teach us valuable lessons, but trusted friends need to be objective about other's problems.

Another error is focusing too much on either comfort or confrontation. Jesus, John told us, embodied both grace and truth. As trusted friends we need to blend heartfelt compassion with courage showing genuine care about the painful reality of a person's life and communicating the clear truth of God's word. "[Speak] the truth in love" (Eph. 4:15).

Psychological instruments gauge the response of people on this scale of compassion and courage. Those who tend to be warm and understanding sometimes need to muster the courage to speak boldly when it's appropriate, and those who naturally tend to give clear directives need to blend those directions with warmth and patience.

Avoid bumper-sticker answers like the plague! People need handles on their complicated situations, but we do them no favors by offering simplistic solutions such as, "Just pray about it," "Jesus is the answer," or "It's not so bad. You'll feel better soon."

Let's examine important elements of responding:

Comforting: In most cases your presence and love provide the most meaningful comfort for a hurting person. Words are secondary. If people cry, let them cry without hurrying them. If they apologize for crying, assure them that their tears are entirely appropriate and you appreciate their trusting you with their hearts.

Perhaps the most comforting realization for people in pain is to know they aren't alone. If the person needs to go to the hospital to visit a sick family member, offer to go along. If he needs to go through the room of a family member who died, offer to accompany him. And if it's not convenient or appropriate to be there in person, give the person your phone number and encourage him or her to call.

Describe a time when you felt comforted by someone.
What did that person do or say that was meaningful to you?

Did

Said

Encouraging: Sue realized it had been one month since Martha's 19-year-old son had been killed in a car accident. She called Martha to remind her that she was still praying for her family. Martha was encouraged by the call because no one seemed to want to talk to her about the loss.

Hurting people desperately need an infusion of hope. Your interest and care provide a wealth of encouragement, and beyond your presence, you can offer messages of affirmation, such as:

"You can do this. I'm sure you can. I'll help you."

"This is hard, but you're learning some of the most valuable lessons in life."

"I'm so proud of you for being honest about what happened to you. You have made tremendous progress, and you're going to make a lot more."

It may sound strange, but you can expect resistance to these words of encouragement. People long to hear them, but pain and hopelessness often erode confidence so much that they simply can't believe anything good will ever happen to them again. If the person responds to your encouragement by shaking her head or with words of doubt, don't argue; just reaffirm your words with warmth and kindness.

Think of times when you felt confused, discouraged, angry, or hurt.
Write some statements or messages that you found encouraging.

List the names of some people in your life who need to hear a message of encouragement from you.

Information: In virtually every relationship as a trusted friend, you have the opportunity to provide important—and perhaps life-changing—insights to the needy person. Some people come to you with rigidly constructed presumptions about the way life works, but in many cases those presumptions are based on twisted logic and lies. And some come to you fresh from experiencing a traumatic event. Their minds are fogged by the devastation, and they can't think clearly enough to sort through the information they receive.

People who have experienced long-term, dysfunctional relationships (abuse, abandonment, addictions, mental illness, rage, adultery, etc.) have survived by creating their own reality that minimizes pain. Their construction of truth has helped them survive, but it's blocked their ability to respond to reality and find genuine help. Now you have the opportunity to communicate truth and clarify the complexities of relationships in these painful, twisted environments.

People who grow up in alcoholic (and other addictive) families live by three simple rules: Don't talk, don't trust, and don't feel. They can talk about anything and everything except "the elephant in the room"—the family member's addiction and the pain they feel. They either trust untrustworthy people who habitually lie to them, or they believe they can't trust anybody. They repress the intense hurt and anger they feel until it explodes, and they feel so guilty that they put the clamps on their emotions even more tightly—until they explode again. As a trusted friend you will only begin the process of helping the family member of an addict begin to embrace the hard realities she has tried to avoid for many years, but a simple explanation of these three rules can be a helpful first step.

Many of those we help are grieving significant losses from death, disease, divorce, or some other painful event. Explaining the stages of grief to these people can help them realize they won't always feel the way they do at that moment. That realization gives them a new sense of hope.

Read John 4:4-10. Describe how Jesus connected with the woman.

Jesus gave her information she needed to hear. What did He say in a way that allowed her to really hear it?

Correction: If we truly love people, we are willing to tell them the truth, and sometimes the truth involves correcting their perspectives, attitudes, or behaviors. We are trusted friends who long for people to walk with God in integrity and strength. When they are going in the wrong direction, we show our love for them by gently and clearly directing them back to God's purpose and path for their lives. We don't demand compliance, and we certainly don't try to manipulate their choices. We simply offer insight about the consequences of their choices and encourage them to make good decisions. Avoid coming across as judge, jury, and executioner.

To the Galatians, Paul wrote, "Brothers, if someone is caught in a sin, you who are spiritual should restore him gently. But watch yourself, or you also may be tempted. Carry each other's burdens, and in this way you will fulfill the law of Christ" (Gal. 6:1-2). We may be horrified at someone's behavior, but we need to keep a lid on our expressions, and we need to communicate with gentleness. The goal, Paul said, isn't exposing, blasting, and condemning the person. It's restoration. He encouraged us to be careful because we may "be tempted." What was he talking about? He was not necessarily implying that we'll be tempted to sin in the same way the person is sinning but that we'll be tempted to respond in a sinful way—condemning, communicating disgust, or running away.

On a scale of 0 (very poorly) to 10 (like Jesus would have done it), how well do you communicate correction with both truth and grace?
_____

What could you do better next time?

REFERRING

In the short-term model we use the first two (and occasionally three) meetings to uncover the issues and provide some feedback. The last meeting is designed to refer the person to a counselor, agency, support group, attorney, or any other resource that's needed.

61

Of course, we need to have an arsenal of trusted, highly recommended resources at our disposal. As you and others receive training and compile names of counselors and other resources, you can add those that prove to be reliable and delete those that are questionable. In most communities, you'll be able to provide the names and contact information for:

- At least one competent, licensed Christian counselor
- At least one trusted psychiatrist
- At least one family practice physician who has spiritual values
- At least one attorney who practices family law
- A reputable funeral home
- Debt counseling resources
- A nursing home
- Meals on Wheels
- Helping Hands
- Crisis Pregnancy Center
- Support groups for alcohol and drug dependency, food disorders, codependence, gambling, and sexual addictions
- Police and fire department.

Next week we'll compile a list of resources. In the meantime, try to remember comments—positive and negative—about resources your friends have used.

When you make a referral, you may be asking people to take one of the most threatening steps in their lives. They have mustered the courage to expose their need to you, and that's a wonderful first step. Going to a doctor, counselor, group, or any other individual or agency requires even more bravery because now they will be asked to make difficult, perhaps excruciating, changes in their lives.

When you make referrals, explain the benefits people will receive. Paint a vision of the future of emotional, physical, relational, or financial health, and encourage people to take the next step to call for an appointment in the next few hours or days.

Don't assume that giving someone a piece of paper with a name and phone number will change a life. In many instances, the "hand off" between your last meeting and the first meeting with the resource simply doesn't happen. Excuses multiply and fear cripples good intentions. If it's appropriate, tell the person you will call in a couple of days to find out when the appointment is scheduled or how the first meeting went.

What might prevent an effective hand-off to a resource?
Underline the ones that seem more important to you.

fear	threat of exposure
poor handwriting	insecurity
lack of trust	unwilling to call or go
thinks he or she can solve it alone	bad hair day
lack of transportation	time off work
timidity	

List one or more factors that can make that hand-off more effective.

CONFIDENTIALITY

When people trust you enough to confide in you, don't betray that trust by gossiping to others or telling about the person in the guise of a prayer request. However, if the person is suicidal, homicidal, or abusive, tell your pastor or a counselor about it. In talking with teenagers, it's a good idea to tell them that anything they say to you might be reported to their parents. You want to help, but it doesn't help anyone when you get caught in a manipulative triangle.

Breaking confidentiality is gossip. The motives are either to hurt the person we gossip about—that's revenge—or to present ourselves as superior to that person. Either way, it's sin.

If you have a concern about someone you assist, talk to your ministry leader in private to get input and assistance. Getting assistance from a person to whom you are accountable isn't gossip, but be careful that you guard another person's secrets and reputation as much as possible.

Read Proverbs 16:28 and 18:8. In your own words describe the motivation of gossip.

Describe the devastation caused by gossip.

For more information about this important topic, read "The Limits of Confidentiality" on page 139 of the Appendix.

A TOUCH OF HUMILITY

Don't assume you're clairvoyant and can "read" people perfectly. Even the most astute counselors are wrong from time to time. People are amazingly complex creatures, and many powerful factors in their lives lay hidden, even from themselves. In the first week we examined many different reasons why people suffer. In addition to our sins, others' sins, natural disasters, and unexplained events, people are afflicted by changing hormones, stages of life and work, and countless other elements of life. Stay humble and realize you may not have all the facts. Even if you did, you may not read them correctly.

Also, don't assume that what you hear from one person in a strained relationship is "the truth, the whole truth, and nothing but the truth." All of us are biased in some way, and we tend to shade the facts to make us look a little better. And sometimes the facts aren't just shaded—they're whitewashed!

A proverb reminds us, "The first to present his case seems right, till another comes forward and questions him" (Prov. 18:17). Listen carefully to the person telling you about a situation, but realize that the person's spouse, child, parent, or friend may have a different story to tell. The short-term model doesn't require you to figure out the truth and convince both sides. Your goal is simply to listen so they feel understood and help them find the best resource available to meet their needs.

On a scale of 0 (not good at all) to 10 (antenna up!), how well do you read people?

0   1   2   3   4   5   6   7   8   9   10
NOT GOOD AT ALL   ANTENNA UP

We tend to believe the person who is in front of us telling his or her story instead of remembering there are always two sides. What are some negative consequences that we might regret when we completely buy the first person's story?

PAY ATTENTION TO GOD AS YOU LISTEN

On page 50 we talked about the complexities of communication. Another layer of complexity occurs when we learn to listen with spiritual ears. Before we talk to someone, we can ask God for wisdom and direction in the conversation, and as the talk progresses, we can be sensitive to the Spirit's nudging. Quite often He reminds us of a passage of Scripture that speaks clearly to the person's predicament, He may bring to mind a situation we've experience that parallels the person's needs, or He may prompt us to pray silently about a particular problem the person brought to the surface.

One of the most powerful concepts in being trusted friends is to realize that *three* are present in any conversation. God may be invisible, but He is present, aware of every need, and willing to participate by imparting truth and grace.

In her book, *Conversation Peace*, Mary Kassian writes:

> I believe that our communication problems are, at their deepest root, spiritual problems. As such, they require spiritual solutions. And for that, we must turn to God. ... For the final word on how to transform our words, the Bible is our book. It sets a high standard for speech and also for thoughts and attitudes. But even more importantly, it reveals the "secret" for how to reach that standard—*power*. God's power. Not some magical formula or phrase. Not the "right" technique or combination of words. ... He has given us *his* Word to transform and revolutionize *our* words and lead us into conversation peace.[1]

When we first learn to be trusted friends, we often focus primarily on principles we've learned so that we can use them effectively. When we've mastered them, we can give more of our attention to people so that we really listen to their hearts' desires. Then, as those skills become second nature, we become more aware of God's gracious presence in the conversation and we look to Him before, during, and after we meet with people.

Even when we aren't consciously aware of God's presence, He's there, guiding us, opening hearts and minds, and changing lives—even ours.

LISTEN OFTEN, LISTEN WELL

In week 3 we learned the five factors in good listening. Some of us are naturally gifted with these skills, but all of us can learn to be more effective. Make a commitment to take the steps you need to be a better listener and trust God to give you success as you seek to listen often and listen well.

We've covered a lot of information this week. Which aspect of being a great listener stood out to you?

What are two steps you can take to be a better listener?

1.

2.

When I talk to one of my family members this week, I will try to

I will try to be comfortable with silence when

1. Mary A. Kassian. *Conversation Peace, Improve Your Relationships One Word at a Time.* (Nashville: Broadman & Holman Publishers, 2004), 2.

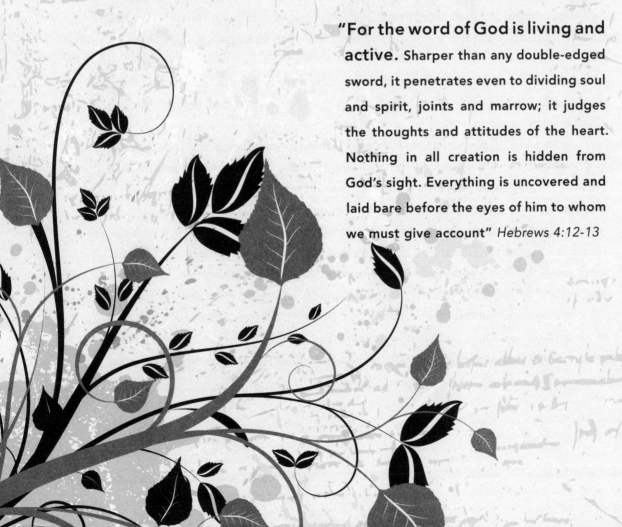

week four

RELYING ON THE SCRIPTURES AND PRAYER

"For the word of God is living and active. Sharper than any double-edged sword, it penetrates even to dividing soul and spirit, joints and marrow; it judges the thoughts and attitudes of the heart. Nothing in all creation is hidden from God's sight. Everything is uncovered and laid bare before the eyes of him to whom we must give account" *Hebrews 4:12-13*

Hurting, confused people desperately need God to touch their lives with His love, truth, and strength. God has given us His Word to comfort and direct us. In our role as trusted friends, we have the privilege of sharing His truth with people to encourage them, guide them, and occasionally correct them.

In addition, God wants each of us to connect with Him in prayer. The powerful combination of God's truth and prayer transforms lives. Those who are emotionally wounded, physically sick, relationally distraught, or financially stuck need us to share God's Word and Model Prayer as we care for them.

CONTEXT AND PERMISSION

When people come to us with a problem (or we learn they have a problem), our first instinct may be to share a passage of Scripture and pray with them. That instinct may be exactly the right thing to do, but not always. Sometimes we have to earn the right to share God's Word and pray with someone. Maybe the person is angry with God, or maybe he or she isn't a Christian and doesn't understand how prayer puts us in touch with the One who meets needs.

Be confident in God's Word and the power of prayer, but be sensitive about when it is appropriate. Without this sensitivity, people who turn to us may feel we are giving them simple answers to complex problems. In fact, some of the people we help come to us with feelings of disappointment and even betrayal by Bible-believing Christians. In those cases bringing out the Bible too quickly can build a wall that may prove to be too high to climb in a few conversations.

As we talk with people outside our church family, among friends or relatives, in our neighborhood, or at work, one of the questions to ask is: "What is your spiritual background?" Many people will give the name of their denomination or the actual church if they attend, so be prepared to ask a follow-up question or two, such as, "How has your spiritual life been meaningful to you in the past?" and "Has your experience with the church been positive?" Regardless of the answer, it's good to continue with, "Tell me more about that." The answers to those questions will help you determine the person's receptiveness to your sharing Scripture and praying or sharing the good news of Christ.

In your conversations listen carefully first and foremost to the person's description of the need or hurt. Don't jump to offer solutions, even if they seem obvious to you. After listening for a long time—for most of the first time you meet—listen especially to the spiritual diagnostic questions. At that point and only if it's appropriate, ask for permission to read a passage of Scripture and/or pray.

For those who have been hurt by Christians and disappointed in their church experience, don't share Scripture yet. Just ask for permission to pray for them. Say something like this: "I'm so sorry that you've been hurt by Christians. I want you to know that I'm not going to pressure you in any way. I want to be your friend. And as your friend, I want you to know that God really does love you, and He cares very much about the situation you're in. Would you mind if I take a minute to pray for you?"

In the vast majority of cases, the person will be happy for you to pray. If he or she declines, don't force it. Just agree with the decision and continue to talk about the next step in the process of discovery.

If you sense that the person would be comforted and encouraged by a passage from God's Word, you can say, "There's a Scripture that has meant a lot to me. Would you mind if I share it with you?" If the person agrees, read the passage and tell how God has used it in your life. Use passages of hope and encouragement, but be careful not to promise more than God intends to deliver. He doesn't guarantee immediate, complete healing or relief.

Sometimes God grants the request for healing, but often He doesn't. Even if He doesn't give the solution quickly, He promises His presence even when we can't sense it, His purpose when we can't seem to find it, and His grace though we don't deserve it. One of the most important insights we can impart to those who suffer is that God wants to use pain, disappointment, pruning, and waiting on God's answers to our prayers to deepen our trust in Him. Of course, no one pursues pain, but if we fail to accept it as God's curriculum to teach us some of the most important lessons we can ever learn, we will miss God's purpose for it.

Read James 1:2-4. What is the goal of our hurts and healing?

In his insightful book *Knowing God,* J. I. Packer observed that God has a higher purpose than helping us avoid pain. "This is what all the work of grace aims at—an even deeper knowledge of God, and an ever closer fellowship with Him. Grace is God drawing us sinners closer and closer to Him.

"How does God in grace prosecute this purpose? Not by shielding us from assault by the world, the flesh, and the devil, nor by protecting us from burdensome and frustrating circumstances, nor yet by shielding us from troubles created by our own temperament and psychology; but rather by exposing us to all these things, so as to overwhelm us with a sense of our own inadequacy, and to drive us to cling to Him more closely. This is the ultimate reason, from our standpoint, why God fills our lives with troubles and perplexities of one sort or another—it is to ensure that we shall learn to hold Him fast."[1]

How has God used pain and waiting in your life as part of His curriculum to teach you to trust him more? Use these experiences to jog your memory: illness, death, injury, betrayal, debt, sterility, image problems, some form of abuse, or dysfunctional family.

Pain

Waiting

THE CALL TO HONESTY

From time to time all of us experience emotional, relational, and spiritual hurts, but if we aren't aware of the extent of our wounds, we can't take steps toward healing and hope. Most often our problem isn't a lack of knowledge about the painful event but a lack of objectivity about the nature of the damage we've experienced.

Objectivity is threatening. To become aware of the depth of our pain causes us to feel out of control, and people will do *almost anything* to keep from feeling that way. We may be driven to prove ourselves to earn respect, or we may try to please people to win approval, or we may give up and hide or numb ourselves with drugs, alcohol, food, or another substance or behavior. Look at the walls these people built around their hurts to keep people from seeing their pain.

- A college student was considered "the life of the party." She was intelligent, witty, and sociable, but when she was by herself, she experienced deep loneliness and seething resentment.

- A businessman who, as a child, was neglected by his ambitious father thought, *If I can just get that promotion, then I'll be happy. Success is what really counts in life!* He received a number of promotions and raises because he was driven to perform well, but happiness continued to elude him.

- A housewife with three children painfully wondered, *Why don't I feel close to my husband?* Having grown up with an alcoholic father and a demanding mother, this woman has never felt lovable, and so she can't receive her husband's love.

- An articulate church leader speaks powerfully about the unconditional love and grace of God, yet he has never understood how to apply his own teaching to his life and relationships.

Read this man's account of his own spiritual journey.

This objective "light" didn't begin to penetrate my own life for many years. Before that time, whenever I felt the pain of rejection, the sting of sarcasm, or anything less than the complete approval of others, I tried to shrug it off. I reasoned that because I was a Christian, I should exude an attitude of happiness and contentment in all things and at all times. When something didn't go the way I'd hoped or planned, I simply told myself it didn't really matter. Though I tried to convince myself that I was doing OK, my gloomy countenance told those who were closest to me another story.

On one such occasion, a good friend of mine inquired about what was wrong. "You seem troubled," he said. "Is anything bothering you?"

"Me? No, I'm fine."

"You don't seem fine to me," he persisted. "You're acting as though you might be depressed about something."

I stuck to my time-tested text. "No, really, I am fine. I guess I've just been a little pressured lately."

The truth was that an idea I'd presented in a business meeting the week before had been challenged and later shot down. I didn't think it really mattered at first, but after hearing my friend's remarks, I began to wonder if I was being honest with myself.

Several weeks later I phoned this friend to thank him for asking about my demeanor. I briefly told him about the business meeting and said, "Realizing I was hurt because my idea was rejected has enabled me to be honest with the Lord about my feelings and begin working through them."

"I'm sorry about what happened," he said, "but I appreciate your honesty and think it's great that you're doing something constructive with a difficult situation."

Over time I began to confide in this friend about other problems I encountered. He helped me a lot. At times, he would say, "Here's how I'd feel in your situation. I'd be angry because … Do you feel angry?" Or, "I'd be hurt because … Do you feel hurt?"

In the light of his honesty and love, and through the gracious work of the Holy Spirit, I began to be honest with myself and with God. The tough exterior I had developed started cracking, and I began to experience the pain I had neither wanted nor allowed myself to feel. This was hardly pleasant, but acknowledging the presence of hurt in my life was my first step toward finding comfort.

The prayers of David show us the importance of being honest with God. Read Psalm 13. Describe how David's mood changed.

From: To:

Read Psalms 40; 42; and 44. List examples of David's honesty with God.

Are you as honest about your feelings? ❑ yes ❑ no

The prayers of Paul give us purpose and direction as we take steps along the path of following Christ. Read Colossians 1:9-14. Which verse means the most to you as you confront everyday difficulties?

THE NEED FOR OBJECTIVITY

Why do people in need (and all of us) often lack objectivity? Why can't we see the reality of our lives? Why are we afraid to "turn on the lights"? There are a number of answers to these questions, and they vary for each person.

Perhaps we think our situations are normal—that experiencing loneliness, hurt, and anger contain all there is to life. Perhaps we want to be good Christians, and believing that good Christians don't have problems or feelings like ours, we deny the existence of our painful emotions.

Perhaps our lack of objectivity is a learned response from childhood. All of us desperately want our parents to be loving and supportive. If ours aren't (or weren't), we may protect our concept of them by blaming ourselves for their lack of love and denying that we have been hurt by their behavior.

Human beings develop elaborate defense mechanisms to block pain and gain significance. We suppress emotions; we try to do everything perfectly; we drive ourselves to succeed, or we withdraw and become passive; we attack people who hurt us; we punish ourselves when we fail; we try to say clever things to be accepted; we help people so that we will be appreciated; and we say and do countless other things.

A sense of need usually propels us to look for an alternative. Perhaps we have the courage to examine ourselves and may desperately want to change, but we may feel unsure of how and where to start. We may refuse to look honestly within due to our fear of what we'll find, or we may be afraid that even if we can discover what's wrong, nothing can help us.

We can't turn on the light of objectivity by ourselves. We need guidance from the Holy Spirit, as well as the honesty, love, and encouragement of at least one other person who's willing to help us. Even then we may become depressed as we begin to discover the effects of our wounds. Some of us have deep emotional and spiritual scars resulting from the neglect, abuse, and manipulation that often accompany living in a dysfunctional family (alcoholism, drug abuse, absent father or mother, excessive anger, verbal and/or physical abuse, and so on), but all of us bear the effects of our own sinful nature and the imperfections of others.

Whether a needy person's hurts are deep or relatively mild, God can use us to help him or her begin to be honest about them. We can provide honesty and affirmation so that healing can begin. Many people mistakenly believe that God doesn't want them to be honest about their sins and pains. If they tell Him how they really feel, they believe God will be upset with them. But the Scriptures tell us that God doesn't want us to be superficial—in our relationship with Him, with others, or in our own lives. David wrote:

> *"Surely you desire truth in the inner parts;*
> *you teach me wisdom in the inmost place" (Ps. 51:6).*

BIBLICAL INSIGHTS

The Lord desires truth and honesty at the deepest level and wants us to experience His love, forgiveness, and power in all areas of our lives. Experiencing His love doesn't mean that all of our thoughts, emotions, and behaviors will be pleasant and pure. It means that we can be real, feeling pain and joy, love and anger, confidence and confusion.

Some of the biblical verses we use most often are the psalms, especially the psalms of David. The psalms give us tremendous insight about what it means to be honest with the Lord. David and other psalmists wrote about the full range of their responses to situations. For example, David expressed his anger with the Lord because he felt abandoned.

> *"I say to God my Rock, 'Why have you forgotten me?'*
> *Why must I go about mourning, oppressed by the enemy?" (Ps. 42:9-10).*

At times David was very angry with others, and he expressed that anger to the Lord in terms that reveal the depth of his feelings:
> *"Break the teeth in their mouths, O God;*
> *tear out, O Lord the fangs of the lions!*
> *Let them vanish like water that flows away;*
> *when they draw the bow, let their arrows be blunted.*
> *Like a slug melting away as it moves along; like a stillborn child,*
> *may they not see the sun.*
> *Before your pots can feel the heat of the thorns—whether*
> *they be green or dry—the wicked will be swept away" (Ps. 58:6-9).*

David wrote of his despair about difficult situations:
> *"My heart is in anguish within me;*
> *the terrors of death assail me.*
> *"Fear and trembling have beset me;*
> *horror has overwhelmed me" (Ps. 55:4-5).*

And he communicated his despair to the Lord:

> *"Why do you hide your face and forget our misery and oppression?*
> *We are brought down to the dust; our bodies cling to the ground"* (Ps. 44:24-25).

Sometimes he was confused:

> *"How long, O Lord? Will you forget me forever?*
> *How long will you hide your face from me?*
> *How long must I wrestle with my thoughts and every day*
> *have sorrow in my heart?"* (Ps. 13:1-2).

Sometimes David expressed his love for the Lord:

> *"As the deer pants for streams of water,*
> *so my soul pants for you, O God.*
> *My soul thirsts for God, for the living God.*
> *When can I go and meet with God?"* (Ps. 42:1-2).

At times, David declared his trust in the Lord:

> *"The Lord is my light and my salvation—*
> *whom shall I fear?*
> *The Lord is the stronghold of my life—*
> *of whom shall I be afraid?*
> *When evil men advance against me to devour my flesh,*
> *when my enemies and my foes attack me,*
> *they will stumble and fall.*
> *Though an army besiege me, my heart will not fear;*
> *though war break out against me, even then I will be confident"* (Ps. 27:1-3).

At other times, he was filled with praise for God:

> *"I will exalt you, my God the King;*
> *I will praise your name forever and ever.*
> *Every day I will praise you and extol your name forever and ever.*
> *Great is the Lord and most worthy of praise;*
> *his greatness no one can fathom"* (Ps. 145:1-3).

These passages demonstrate that God, who spoke of David as a man after His own heart, wants us to be open and honest with Him about all of our emotions, not just the pleasant ones.

Be prepared to share with your group Scriptures God has used to help you be honest about pain and disappointment, as well as thankfulness and praise.

On a scale of 0 (not) to 10 (completely), how would you rate yourself in being honest with God about your feelings?

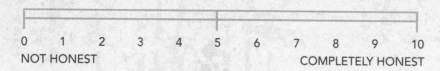

```
 0    1    2    3    4    5    6    7    8    9    10
NOT HONEST                        COMPLETELY HONEST
```

What steps do you need to take (if any) to move up the scale of honesty and intimacy with God? (Check one or more.)

❑ spend more time in the Word
❑ write my feelings in a journal
❑ trust God won't reject my feelings
❑ find an objective Christian to listen
❑ honestly talk to God about my feelings
❑ enlist others to pray for me
❑ other

Some people can read passages like those in the Book of Psalms and begin moving toward healing and health rather quickly. Others, however, may read and study, go to seminars and meetings, and still feel depressed. They may even be in relationships where they are loved and encouraged, but they may not see substantive change in their lives and patterns of behavior.

One reason for this spiritual and emotional inertia is a sense of hopelessness. For various reasons (family background, past experiences, poor modeling), we may have negative presumptions, which determine our receptivity to love and truth.

In some cases God's light may have revealed our pain and wall of defenses, but it may not yet have penetrated to our deepest thoughts and beliefs about ourselves. These beliefs may not be clearly articulated, but often reflect misperceptions such as these:

- God doesn't really care about me.
- I'm an unlovable, worthless person. Nobody will ever love me.
- I'll never be able to change.
- I've been a failure all my life. I guess I'll always be a failure.
- If people really knew me, they wouldn't like me.

When the painful light of love and honesty shines on thoughts of hopelessness, we begin to admit that we really do feel negatively about ourselves—and have for a long time. But God's love, expressed through trusted friends and woven into people's lives by His Spirit and His Word, can bring healing even to the deepest wounds over a period of time.

If you share Bible passages that have been meaningful to you with a hurting, discouraged person, what are some responses you might expect from him or her? Circle your answers.

insight	resistance	apathy
emotions	anger	questions
peace	disbelief	hope

In the Appendix you will find a list of Scriptures to share with those who need encouragement or answers clearly spelled out in the Bible. See pages 128-129.

WHO WE ARE IN CHRIST

All of us have favorite passages from the Bible, ones God has used to encourage us in the most difficult times in our lives. These give us hope when we had been hopeless and light when we only saw darkness. Many hurting people need to be reminded of who they have become as Christ's grace and mercy led them to salvation.

If someone asked, "Who are you?" how would you answer? We usually think of our identity in terms of our function in society. We say, "I'm a salesman." "I'm a mother of three boys." "I'm a lawyer … a student … a secretary." Or maybe we would say, "I'm an American … a Republican … a Democrat … a Christian."

When the apostle John wanted to identify himself in his Gospel, he referred to himself as the disciple whom Jesus loved (John 13:23; 21:7,20). John's sense of being loved and accepted by Christ was so strong that this was how he identified himself.

When Paul wrote to the churches, he put a great deal of emphasis on teaching the believers about their identity. As a general rule, the first half of each letter is about identity; the second half contains specific applications of that identity. His letter to the believers in Ephesus is particularly instructive. The first three chapters clearly explain our identity in Christ. Let's take a look at part of the first chapter:

> *"Praise be to the God and Father of our Lord Jesus Christ, who has blessed us in the heavenly realms with every spiritual blessing in Christ. For he chose us in him before the creation of the world to be holy and blameless in his sight. In love he predestined us to be adopted as his sons through Jesus Christ, in accordance with his pleasure and will—to the praise of his glorious grace, which he has freely given us in the One he loves. In him we have redemption through his blood, the forgiveness of sins, in accordance with the riches of God's grace that he lavished on us with all wisdom and understanding. … And you also were included in Christ when you heard the word of truth, the gospel of your salvation. Having believed, you were marked in him with a seal, the promised Holy Spirit, who is a deposit guaranteeing our inheritance until the redemption of those who are God's possession—to the praise of his glory" (Eph. 1:3-8,13-14).*

Several key words in this passage relate to our identity in Christ:

God has chosen us: But why? Were we chosen because we are smart, good-looking, rich, efficient, or some other trait? No, we have been chosen so that we can be declared holy and blameless before Him: not perfect in our behavior, but secure in our identity.

God has adopted us: We usually use the term *child of God* without thinking about it, but He didn't have to adopt us. He could have left us as helpless and hopeless people, or He could have made us His slaves. Instead, He adopted us like the Romans adopted a person, as an adult child with full privileges as an heir.

As Christians, we have been forgiven: Christ's death is the complete payment for our sins. Those wrongs that condemn us as guilty before God have been paid in full.

We are not just excused and our sins waved off by a benevolent grandfather figure. These sins demand payment, the awful payment of Christ's death on the cross. How much are we forgiven? The verse says according to the riches of His grace. There is no sin too great, no offense too bad (except refusing to accept Christ's payment for sin) that it is unforgivable.

We've been sealed by the Holy Spirit: The seal of Rome signified ownership and security. When Christ was put in the tomb, the Pharisees asked Pilate to make it secure so no one could steal the body and say that Jesus was raised from the dead. That seal was the ultimate in Roman security, yet it could not keep Christ from His resurrection.

Paul used the idea of a seal to express the believer's security in Christ. The Holy Spirit's seal is the ultimate in spiritual security, but unlike the Roman seal, it cannot be broken. This seal signifies that we have been bought by the blood of Christ (1 Cor. 6:19-20), so we are owned by God. Also, it means that we are secure in our relationship with Him. If we have trusted in Christ as our Savior and have experienced His forgiveness and adoption, then He will never drop us, lose us, or reject us.

Paul wrote to the believers in Rome: "For I am convinced that neither death nor life, neither angels nor demons, neither the present nor the future, nor any powers, neither height nor depth, nor anything else in all creation, will be able to separate us from the love of God that is in Christ Jesus our Lord" (Rom. 8:38-39).

Give an example of a way to weave prayer and Scriptures together in your conversations with a hurting person?

What factors determine the effectiveness of this effort?

THE IMPORTANCE OF PRAYER

People in the first century churches were just like us: They experienced great joys of seeing God work, and they suffered the painful effects of sin, shame, heartache, confusion, bitterness, and broken relationships. As Paul wrote to believers, he expressed prayers that God would give people wisdom, courage, and strength to do God's will in every circumstance. For example, he asked God to enable the Philippians' love to "abound more and more in knowledge and depth of insight, so that you may be able to discern what is best and may be pure and blameless until the day of Christ" (Phil. 1:9-10).

To the Colossians he wrote a prayer asking God to fill them "with the knowledge of his will through all spiritual wisdom and understanding … being strengthened with all power according to his glorious might so that you may have great endurance and patience, and joyfully giving thanks to the Father" (Col. 1:9,11-12).

As you read Paul's letters, remember that his written prayers asked God to intervene in the lives of people who are just like those who accept your offer for help. Our friends, like the first-century believers, desperately need God to break through their confusion and pain to give them assurance of his forgiveness, hope, and strength.

PATTERNS OF PRAYER

As you prepare for a conversation with someone:

- **Pray for yourself:** Ask God to give you wisdom, compassion, direction, and insight to uncover the often underlying issues and the ability to listen carefully.

- **Pray for the person:** Thank God for the person's willingness to seek help, and ask God to give this person clarity to see the real issues and courage to take action. Use Paul's prayers as models for your requests for the person you seek to help.

- **Pray for the conversation:** Trust God to direct you in the course of the conversation, to remind you of things the person has told you so you can "connect the dots" and make sense of the situation. Trust God's Spirit to give the person the light of insight, the hope for change, and the courage to take necessary steps.

Remember that the battle is not with "flesh and blood" but with the forces of darkness that want to keep people locked in the dungeon of bitterness, shame, and passivity. Satan uses weapons of temptation, accusation, and confusion, but we trust in God's powerful Word and His Spirit to win those battles.

"For though we live in the world, we do not wage war as the world does. The weapons we fight with are not the weapons of the world. On the contrary, they have divine power to demolish strongholds. We demolish arguments and every pretension that sets itself up against the knowledge of God, and we take captive every thought to make it obedient to Christ" (2 Cor. 10:3-5).

As we talk with struggling people, they often think God has abandoned them, or they believe they've done something that prevents them from experiencing the grace and power of God. These are, in Paul's words, "strongholds" of doubt and false "pretensions" about the character of God. We have the privilege to partner with the Word of God and the Spirit of God to "demolish" those strongholds and correct the false pretensions about God's love and purposes. Prayer is a powerful weapon in this fight.

In your conversations as a trusted friend, pray with and for people. At the close of conversations, you can simply ask, "Would it be OK if I pray for you?" In the vast majority of cases, people will be happy for you to pray for them. At this moment, avoid simplistic prayers and promises that "everything will turn out all right." God often has more important purposes than simply giving us relief. Instead, put the problems you've discussed in the hands of God, reflect on His love and power, and acknowledge that His purposes include using problems to strengthen our faith, deepen our dependence, and sharpen our understanding of His ways. And ask God to give the person clarity of direction and courage to act.

Describe your pattern of praying.

- ❑ I pray for an immediate solution.
- ❑ I pray for a specific answer.
- ❑ I pray that everything will turn out all right.

Other_____

In the course of conversations sometimes it's appropriate to stop and pray for the person or about a situation right then. Ask for permission to pray, seeking God for His comfort and a fresh sense of hope.

As you express your dependence on God in prayer, you'll be a wonderful model for the person you are helping. Perhaps no one else in that person's life is truly seeking God's wisdom, power, and purposes. As you verbalize your trust that God is loving, powerful, sovereign, and kind, the person will gain a glimpse of what it means to trust God with life's biggest problems.

SHARING THE GOOD NEWS

Some studies estimate that half of the people who attend church each Sunday are not sure of their salvation. That figure varies by denomination and by individual churches, but it's safe to say that not everybody who comes to us, from the church or the community, has experienced God's transforming grace.

In your conversations, as you ask the spiritual diagnostic questions and you find out the person isn't a believer or is unsure of his or her faith in Christ, ask if you have permission to ask a couple of questions. If the person agrees, you can say something like this: "There are a couple of questions that help people uncover what they believe about God. The first one is: If you were to die today, how sure are you—on a scale of 0 to 100 percent—that you'd go to heaven?" Let the person respond, and then continue: "If you died today and stood before God and He asked, 'Why should I let you into heaven?' how would you respond to Him?"

The answers to those two questions tell you what a person is trusting in, if anything. At that point share your testimony of how you became a Christian. Then ask, "Would you mind if I share with you some things about how to have a relationship with God and know your sins are forgiven and you have eternal life?" If the person agrees, share the gospel with clarity, warmth, and boldness.

Most Christians prefer to use a plan or a gospel tract at this point. If you are using "The Roman Road," for example, mark those passages in your Bible with instructions on where the next verse is found (Go to Rom. 3:23). This approach is called a marked New Testament.

If you are using a tract such as "The Four Spiritual Laws," ask the person to read the tract aloud. When he or she is finished, ask two follow-up questions. First, is there any reason why you could not pray the sinner's prayer right now? If not, would you like to? Then encourage them to repeat the sinner's prayer and invite Jesus to be Lord and Savior today. Always ask the person to repeat after you or read the prayer aloud.

There is no magic prayer. Whatever words you or they use, the words don't save the person. God, who knows our hearts, is the only rightful judge. Be sure to have the person write the date of his or her conversion and sign the tract, Bible, or whatever follow-up materials you may provide.

You might want to use an outline to help you remember key words of a gospel presentation. One way is the ABCs of salvation (see p. 142).

see p. 142

A–I admit that I am a sinner.

B–I believe that Jesus died on the cross to save me from my sins.

C–I confess my sins and ask for Your forgiveness.

Often people will express emotion at this point. Don't call attention to tears or other signs of brokenness. On the other hand, if there is no emotion, don't worry about it. Being saved is a decision we make with our will.

Many people roll along without God in their lives until a tragedy strikes. At that point they realize their desperate need for a Savior, and they are open to the gospel. We will have the incredible joy of being in the right place at the right time to lead many of them to Christ.

Have you had the pleasure of sharing the good news with a friend?
❏ no ❏ yes ❏ I'm waiting for the right time.

What additional information or training do you need to effectively communicate the message of Christ?

Where can you find resources you can use such as tracts, marked Bibles, or a visual story cloth?

Try to stop and pray for the person or about a situation right then. For example, if the person is overcome with sorrow and begins to weep, you might ask for permission to pray, seeking God for His comfort and a fresh sense of hope.

As you express your dependence on God in prayer, you will be a wonderful model for the person you are helping. Perhaps no one else in that person's life is truly seeking God's wisdom, power, and purposes. As you verbalize your trust that God is loving, powerful, sovereign, and kind, the person will gain a glimpse of what it means to trust God with life's biggest problems.

REPRESENTING GOD

When people muster the courage to talk to us about their problems, most of them are "harassed and hopeless, like sheep without a shepherd" (Matt. 9:36). They have lost hope in God, and they don't understand how God's truth and power can work in their difficult situations.

In our role as trusted friends, we have the incredible privilege of representing God to them. In that role, we need to be sensitive, gentle, self-disclosing, and warm as we share truth that God has used in our lives and we take people to the throne of God in prayer.

What have you learned about using prayer and Scriptures in helping people? Share your answer with your small group.

---

1. J. I. Packer. *Knowing God* (Downer's Grove: IL: InterVarsity Press, 1973), 227.

week five

PROVIDING REFERRAL SOURCES

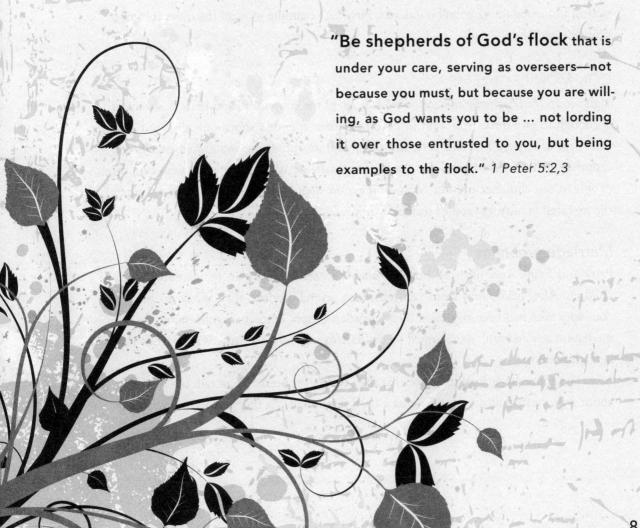

"Be shepherds of God's flock that is under your care, serving as overseers—not because you must, but because you are willing, as God wants you to be ... not lording it over those entrusted to you, but being examples to the flock." *1 Peter 5:2,3*

In week 4 we learned skills in active listening. Some of the people who come to us simply need a friend with a listening ear. In two or three conversations we help them sort out the confusion in their lives and provide enough hope and direction for them to take the next steps on their own. Perhaps they are trying to solve a problem, decide on a course of action, or talk about a loss such as a mate or child, an accident, a job layoff, or effects of a lingering illness. We can help them to grieve so they can resolve their pain and find hope again. In these cases, listening is the best thing you can do. Don't jump in with a "solution" or advice.

But many people need more than a few conversations. They need professional care or long-term assistance from a group or agency. The ability to refer people to competent, trusted professionals is an essential part of being a trusted friend. After listening carefully to help the person feel understood and to discern the heart of the problem, the trusted friend's role is to refer the person to the counselor, group, or agency that can provide specific, professional care for as long as it's needed.

This week we'll examine the problems most people encounter, how to find good resources, and how to make the referral. In addition, we'll look at the importance of setting and maintaining good boundaries. First, let's examine some of the most common problems we'll face.

COMMON PROBLEMS

A glance at *The Diagnostic and Statistical Manual* of the American Psychiatric Association is enough to give those who want to become trusted friends a shock of reality and cold feet. Page after page lists and describes the symptoms of all the recognized psychiatric disorders. Trusted friends, though, are not psychiatrists. We are shepherds who care for people in our churches and our communities. We aren't professionals, but we are often the first step in hurting people's search for hope.

Marriage problems

Patty and Frank were divorced but still unable to settle on a plan for parenting their children. After being away from each other for several months, they agreed to go to a counselor who had been suggested by a Christian couple in their neighborhood. In this mediation session Frank was alarmed by the darts being slung by Patty. Was he really that bad a husband?

The counselor helped them see that they had never been able to talk to each other about a problem that didn't end up as a nasty argument. As they learned principles of communication and listening, their relationship began to improve. Although each had to make concessions, the new parenting agreement worked well

Some people come to us when they learn of a spouse's adultery or addiction to pornography. Others come because they are considering divorce, and some come after they've gone through a divorce. Often they feel like colossal failures.

Think about your friends and family. What are some of the most common causes of problems in their marriages?

Dr. Les Parrott, an author and professor of Christian counseling, observed that the vast majority of trouble in marriages stems from four areas: finances, sex, children, and in-laws. Most marriages struggle with these issues at some point in the relationship, and many strain under the weight of multiple issues at the same time. These four topics, then, form a grid for understanding the complexity of problems when you talk to an individual or a couple struggling with a strained marriage.

Parenting

Roger and Ann had a child diagnosed with ADHD. As the child's symptoms became more noticeable, they felt trapped between acknowledging the diagnosis or pretending everything was OK. "He's just being a boy," Roger would say to others.

One morning Ann got a call from her son's first-grade teacher. Was it the dreaded call she had feared? "Mrs. Boynton, I have good news for you. I have a son with ADHD. I wanted to tell you that Tony not only graduated from high school and college but he's now pursuing a master's degree. I thought maybe you and your husband would be encouraged by my call."

Ann immediately set up a parent conference, and after several months had learned many skills in dealing with her son. A Christian teacher reached out to this family because she had been in the same situation and wanted to help. She became a true trusted friend.

Don't assume that a child's struggles are necessarily the result of poor parenting. Children, and especially teenagers, can be out of control for many reasons. Quite often parental permissiveness or harsh treatment exasperates children, but children are free, moral agents and can make wrong choices. Even the best parents can have a child who makes terrible decisions when influenced by peers or hormones. Always see a child's problem as the whole family's problem. Both parents need to be brought into the search for answers, either at the early stage with you or with a counselor.

Read Colossians 3:21 and Ephesians 6:4. What are some ways fathers and mothers embitter and exasperate their children?

Blended families often create tremendous tension because virtually every person comes to the table with deep hurts and shattered expectations. Trying to put two families together can be explosive. With more than half of adults in our country living as single adults, the difficulty of rearing children in a one-parent family is compounded by only one income.

Depression, Addictions, and Abuse

Doctors recognize many different types of depression. Two large categories are exogenous depression, which is a reaction to real or imagined loss or trauma, and endogenous depression, which is caused by imbalances in body chemistry. In many cases exogenous depression has a relatively short duration and can be resolved with or without medication. Endogenous depression persists for a much longer duration and resists treatment. Bipolar depression consists of periods of "highs" in which the person is unusually optimistic and energetic, often going for days without sleep, then followed by "lows" of depression.[1]

The stresses of life increase anxiety, erode our confidence, and chip away at our physical health, leaving us vulnerable to depression. Stress management, then, is as important as grieving the pain from the loss. Medications can play a useful role in clearing thinking processes so people can make progress in dealing with the issues that caused their depression, but medications provide just one part of the treatment plan. Counselors and doctors work together to bring the right solutions for each person suffering from depression.

In many cases depression is compounded by other serious difficulties including compulsive and addictive behaviors. Also, people who have experienced emotional, physical, or sexual abuse repress their hurt and anger to try to cope with the pain, but sooner or later the crushing weight of shame and hopelessness can drive them into depression. Of course, not every depressed person is an addict or a victim of abuse, but conversely, many addicts (and their family members) and abuse victims become depressed at some time in their lives.

Read Psalm 13. How does this psalm describe the emotional pain and hopelessness of a person experiencing depression? Select several words and write them here or underline them in your Bible.

Debt

More than ever consumer debt hangs like a dark cloud over the lives of millions of people, including Christians. The insatiable thirst for a higher standard of living overwhelms common sense, so people spend beyond their means. The pressure to have more stuff compounds the strain of figuring out how to pay the bills—or which bills to pay—each month. Juggling credit card balances isn't a sport for many people; it's a way of life. The strain of debt causes people to be preoccupied with money instead of relaxing, enjoying relationships, and being thankful for all God has given them.

Debt consumes a person's thoughts, erodes his zeal for Christ, and damages his most treasured relationships. Looking at your own life, write T or F beside each statement.

___ I can trust God to meet my financial needs.
___ You (your spouse) got us into this mess.
___ If God were fair, I would have gotten that promotion and perks.
___ I feel robbed by a stingy God who deprives me of the good life.
___ I know I should be giving to my church and plan to do so once these necessities are taken care of.
___ Even when my faith is weak, God provides what we need.

Vocational problems

Some of us enjoy our work, but many people dread the office and just endure each day. The lack of fulfillment can result from a number of causes: a poor job fit, conflict with the employer or fellow employees, the prospect of layoffs, unrealistic expectations, and travel schedules. Even the good news of promotions and raises increase stress because the company's expectations rise with the salary level.

Read Colossians 3:22-25. How might Paul's admonition to slaves apply to people who struggle with their jobs or unemployment?

Death

All of us encounter situations when someone has lost a family member or close friend and needs some caring concern. Sometimes death comes to those who have lived long, rich, and full lives, but it can also smash into our lives in unexpected tragedies. In our culture most of us remain far removed from the daily reported deaths in so many countries around the world, so death seems odd, out of place, and unexpected. Pain, suffering, and death are unwelcome intruders on our neat, clean, well-ordered lives, so most of those who are left behind don't know how to grieve. Trusted friends are privileged to assist them—even to grieve with them.

Recall funerals or wakes from your parent's generation. What are some ways modern technology and medicine have insulated us from the reality of death?

These advances help us, but they can prevent us from dealing with reality. Read John 11:1-44, focusing on verses 32-36. How did Jesus respond to Lazarus's death? (check)

❑ Jesus wept.
❑ Jesus experienced deep sorrow.
❑ Jesus wanted them to see God's glory.
❑ Death did not defeat Jesus' power.

Mental illness

For thousands of years people have identified unusual behavior as mental illness. Today physicians have categorized these disorders and described them in great detail. Revolutionary technology of brain scans has shed new light on how these disorders disrupt normal brain functioning. Diagnosing mental illness requires years of training in psychiatry or psychology. Don't jump to conclusions when you suspect someone may have a mental illness, and avoid labeling anyone with your own diagnosis. In most cases, the family members of those who are mentally ill need the help of a trusted friend to cope with the confusion and heartache it may bring.

> What damaging consequences occur when we jump to conclusions and label people?

Physical illness

Many individuals and families have to cope with sicknesses: chronic, acute, and terminal. Every person in the family is affected when someone is seriously ill, but they can be so preoccupied with caring for the sick person that they don't think of asking for help. In many cases care is provided for a couple of weeks by a class or small group, but soon the casseroles and visits cease, and people are left to cope by themselves. In our general population medicine has made remarkable advances so that people are living longer. Care for the aging is a genuine need in our communities and our churches. On the other end of the spectrum, advances in reproductive therapies have given hope to tens of thousands of couples who want to have a child. Still, infertility and miscarriages cause intense—but often silent—suffering.

> Read 2 Corinthians 12:8-10. Is it right to pray for healing?
> ❏ yes ❏ no
>
> Does God always heal?
> ❏ yes ❏ no
>
> How should we feel when our prayers for healing aren't answered immediately?

WHEN AND HOW TO REFER

Alice's husband stayed up late every night logged on to the computer. He told her he was doing research for work, so night after night she went to bed without him. But after months of this pattern of behavior, she became suspicious. The next day she checked the computer's cache and found he had been looking at pornography for hours every night. When he came home from work that day, she exploded with hurt and anger, but then she withdrew and became silent. For weeks she bottled up her rage and her sense of being betrayed. Finally, a friend named Beth noticed Alice's generally angry mood. Beth asked what was wrong, but Alice just said, "Oh, it's nothing."

Another week went by, but Beth asked again. This time Alice's façade cracked a little, and she mentioned that her husband was having problems.

Beth asked, "What kind of problems?"

"Oh, you know," Alice replied.

"No, actually I don't," Beth said patiently, "but I'd be glad to listen. Would you like to go to my house where we can talk?"

Alice was reluctant, but she decided to go with her friend. Beth's authentic love and patience gave Alice permission to open the door to the pain in her heart. Beth asked Alice to talk to their pastor, and reluctantly, Alice agreed. That afternoon the two women met with their pastor, and Alice told him about her husband's problem with pornography.

In that conversation Alice talked even more about the impact of her husband's lies, his withdrawal from their children, her loneliness, and her suspicions of other sinful behavior. The pastor immediately took steps to call her husband and set up a meeting the next day. When they met, initial denials were followed by confessions, and within days, Alice and her husband were in marriage counseling.

A few weeks later God worked in Alice's husband's heart, and he realized he needed to be forgiven by his wife and by God. That day he began a new relationship with God and with his wife. However he knew it would take time to rebuild Alice's trust.

Beth related, "All I did was ask a friend how she was doing, but God knew what she needed. I'm so happy for them, and I'm so happy God let me play a small part in their reconciliation." Her part may have been small, but it was crucial.

How does Beth illustrate the process of the short-term model
and appropriate referral?

First meeting:

Second meeting:

Third meeting:

Referral:

The short-term model encourages referral to a professional counselor, agency, or another resource as soon as you have listened, provided emotional support, and discerned the actual nature of the need. A referral can be made **after the first** meeting if you have enough information and the person needs immediate help, **after the second** if you then discern the problem clearly, and **in the third** meeting as a general rule.

If you meet with someone who, after a meeting or two, wants to bring a spouse or child to the next meeting, you might extend the model to include a fourth time together, but this should be an exception to the rule. Watch out for triangling—where you find yourself as referee and then sometimes become part of the problem by taking sides.

If a person is violent or, in your estimation, potentially violent, call 911 for immediate help. Also call your pastor to give the details of the situation and ask for assistance. This step should also be used in a threatened suicide or other harm to a person's body.

When you refer someone:

1. Find the best options available.

Sometimes a gifted counselor doesn't have openings, so in consultation with the person in need, determine if the wait is worth it or if another available counselor is a better choice. Look for a counselor, treatment program, attorney, or agency that specializes in the type of care that's needed. For instance, some counselors are licensed in marriage and family counseling and some in addiction counseling. Some specialize in care for adolescents and others in family systems or another specialty. If the person is depressed or showing other signs of stress, recommend a check up with a physician.

2. Describe the benefits of the resource.

If possible, describe how that person has helped others (without giving names and details, of course). Paint a picture of hope and health for the person you are referring. Explain what you hope God will do in that person's life as a result of going to that resource.

3. Give the resource's contact information in writing.

Include any additional information that might be needed such as office hours, the name of the receptionist, directions to the office, and the particular person in the practice you recommend.

4. Assure the person that you will remain a trusted friend.

However, your role will be secondary in the future. The specialist will provide the primary care. Become concerned if the friend discontinues a treatment plan.

5. Answer any questions the person may have—and there may be quite a few!

What might cause referred people to "fall through the cracks" so that they don't actually make contact and get the help they need?

Avoid these errors or misunderstandings by calling the day of the appointment to verify the place and time. Arrange for child care if the normal provider isn't available. Be prepared to furnish transportation, accompany them to the referral as emotional support, and see that a follow-up visit is scheduled.

ESTABLISHING A RESOURCE NETWORK

One of the most important tasks of a trusted friend is to do the research of screening possible resources to see which ones are (1) reliable, (2) Christ-centered (or at least value Christian beliefs even if they don't share them), (3) available, and (4) targeted to specific needs. Ask your pastor, church staff, friends, counselors, attorneys, and agencies for recommendations. Before long you'll have a working list that you can use with those who need help. You can add to your network those who meet your criteria for excellence and delete those who don't measure up or recommend them with appropriate cautions.

Write the names of resources you already know in each area of need and/or write the names of others who can provide recommendations.

General Christian counseling

Marriage and family counseling

Addiction counseling (possibly by specialty: drugs and alcohol, eating disorders, compulsive gambling, sexual addiction)

A psychiatrist

A drug and alcohol treatment facility

A family practice where children are a part of the therapeutic process

An internal medicine physician who has spiritual values

An attorney who practices family law

A reputable funeral home

Debt counseling resources

A nursing home

Meals on Wheels

Helping Hands

Support groups for alcohol and drug dependency, food disorders, codependence, gambling, and sexual addictions

Police and fire department

Crisis Pregnancy Center

Others who can recommend additional resources

USING THE NETWORK EFFECTIVELY

The effectiveness of your role as a trusted friend depends, in large measure, on the quality of the resources to which you refer people. For that reason your group needs to become an expert in identifying, screening, and selecting the best resources available in your area. Smaller communities, however, don't have as many resources, and some don't have many that value Christ. In those cases you'll have to select the counselor, physician, attorney, or agency that can help most effectively, but prepare people by explaining that they will need to find Christ-centered support from the church instead of from the professional resource. If a city is nearby, check their resources. It would be worth the trip.

You may want to develop a questionnaire to use with counselors to determine their field of expertise and their compatibility with your biblical values. Some questions you can ask include:

1. What type of state license have you earned?
2. How long have you been a counselor?
3. What are your areas of expertise?
4. What age levels do you work with most often?
5. Who are three references you will give me?
6. Do you value the spiritual life of those you counsel? If so, how do you show that you value their relationship with God?
7. Are you a Christian? If so, what role does your faith play in your counseling with clients?
8. In what ways do you use the Bible (if at all) with those you counsel?

9. In what ways do you use prayer (if at all) with those you counsel?

10. Do you encourage people to join support groups? If so, which ones? Where are they located? What feedback do you get from those you've sent there?

11. Who are the professional counselors to whom you refer people for particular diagnoses?

12. Who are the physicians and psychiatrists to whom you refer people if they need medical or mental health care?

THE MATTHEW 18 MODEL

Jackie had put up with Bill's drinking for years. Occasionally, she tried to talk to him about it, but he either blew her off with a dismissive laugh or blew up denying he had a problem. In the past several months, however, Bill was coming home later several nights a week, and their two sons noticed that their dad snapped at them when they did anything that displeased him. Jackie kept thinking things would get better, that Bill would go back to the way things used to be when his drinking only hurt their marriage and not the children. But nothing changed.

Jackie realized that their marriage was barren and the boys were suffering. Something had to change, but she was afraid to say anything. After all, her pleading and insisting hadn't worked before. What would be different now?

A few weeks later, she had had enough. Jackie mustered the courage to confront Bill the morning after he had come in late, obviously drunk, and had yelled at the boys for leaving a toy in the hall. True to form, he interrupted her and yelled, "I don't need your complaining all the time!" And he stormed out the door.

Jackie called two of Bill's friends, men who used to party with Bill but had sobered up in a church-sponsored support group for alcoholics, and she asked them to come to her house that night. She explained about Bill's drinking and her heartache, and they agreed to come. Bill came in around 9, and the two friends knocked on the door a few minutes later. Together, Jackie and the two men spoke the truth to Bill about the damage he was inflicting on his wife and children.

Bill was furious. When the men left, he grabbed his pillow and blanket to sleep on the sofa that night. The next day one of the men went to the bar where Bill often went after work, and he talked to him again about turning his life over to God and getting help for his problem. This time Bill seemed to listen a little more.

The friend met with Bill several times over the next few weeks, and then Bill showed up at the support group. His friend became his sponsor.

Today few churches practice church discipline. Some have policies in place, but church leaders seldom if ever even consider the possibility of following the process Jesus outlined in Matthew 18:15-17:

> *"If your brother sins against you, go and show him his fault, just between the two of you. If he listens to you, you have won your brother over. But if he will not listen, take one or two others along, so that 'every matter may be established by the testimony of two or three witnesses.' If he refuses to listen to them, tell it to the church; and if he refuses to listen even to the church, treat him as you would a pagan or a tax collector."*

God established this process to correct wayward people and to protect those who have been hurt and those who might be hurt by another's sins. It includes four distinct steps:

1. Matthew 18:15. The offended person initiates a face-to-face conversation with the offender. The problem can be resolved at this early stage if the offender admits his sin, asks for forgiveness, and offers any needed restitution; if both people admit errors and ask for forgiveness; or if they realize the problem stems from a misunderstanding, not a sin.

2. Matthew 18:16. If the offender doesn't respond with contrition and repentance to the first encounter, the offended person is instructed to ask two or three witnesses to join in confronting the offender. These witnesses shouldn't simply be supportive friends of the offended person. They need to be actual witnesses of the sin. If the person responds with genuine repentance, the witnesses can help facilitate a reconciliation of the parties.

3. Matthew 18:17a. If the offender doesn't respond positively to the witnesses and the offended person, they should contact the leaders of the church. Now the matter becomes more public as the leaders conduct a hearing to listen to both sides. They then deliberate and rule on the issue. (The church leaders should clearly understand the spiritual and legal procedures to minimize liability to the church. At some point in the membership process, new members should be informed of the policies and procedures of church discipline. This minimizes risk to the church.)

4. Matthew 18:17b. If the offending person is unrepentant during or after the meeting with the church leaders, he is to be treated as an unbeliever. The person is notified in writing by one of the leaders that his behavior is unacceptable to God

and to the church, so they are taking the painful but necessary step of removing the person from membership. This action, it is hoped, will result in the person's repentance and restoration. Then, in a meeting of church members, the church family can be informed of the action regarding that person, without sharing the details of the offense.

People need instruction and encouragement to pray for the person and love him into repentance if possible. They should not, however, excuse the person's behavior or undermine the process the leaders have taken. The goal of this process isn't revenge; it's restoration. The leaders need to be prepared for many questions, misunderstanding, and a process of grieving by the church family.

Church discipline begins with a person-to-person exchange, and it only escalates if repentance isn't demonstrated. The behavior that can prompt disciplinary action includes private and public offenses, divisiveness, slander, moral and ethical lapses, and false teaching. Few cases reach beyond the second stage of witnesses, but few churches teach their people even this simple procedure.

As a trusted friend, talk to your pastor about this issue to learn about policies and procedures in your church. Express your confidence in God and the church leaders to work with you when and if church discipline is necessary, and trust God to lead you when you talk to people who have been deeply hurt by a family member, friend, or church member. The process of church discipline may be one of the most important and powerful tools of being a trusted friend to hurting people.

The process of church discipline can assist you in helping restore relationships torn apart by deception, abuse, moral lapses, abandonment, or false teaching. Find out your church's polices and procedures regarding this issue. Write them here and share them with your group.

Recall a circumstance you've encountered in which church discipline would have been appropriate.

BOUNDARIES

You want to be a trusted friend because you genuinely care about people, but compassionate people often have difficulty recognizing the limitations of their responsibilities in relationships. Needy people want—and often demand—all of you, all the time. Dependence, however, is not healthy for them or for you.

In his letter to the Galatians, Paul gave both sides of compassion and healthy boundaries. He wrote, "Carry each other's burdens, and in this way, you will fulfill the law of Christ." Only a couple of sentences later, he wrote, "for each one should carry his own load" (Gal. 6:2,5). The burden Paul described is a crushing, heavy weight that no one can carry alone, but the load is like a backpack. Paul was telling us that we all need to take responsibility for the normal choices in life (our "load"), but there are times when the "burdens" of life are so heavy that people need help. One of our tasks as trusted friends is to make sure we carry our own loads and take care of ourselves mentally, physically, emotionally, and spiritually. We simply can't be and do what everyone wants from us.

Approximately 80 percent of people in helping professions have a compulsion to rescue people and fix their problems. You may ask: Isn't helping people a good thing? Yes, but compulsions aren't. When we get our identity from people who appreciate our help, we run the risk of blurring the lines of responsibility and doing too much for them so they'll think well of us.

Those of us who have a wounded sense of identity have difficulty taking responsibility for our own needs, but we are overly responsible to fix the needs of others. We serve tirelessly—to the point of exhaustion. We feel that we have to fix people's problems, so we play the role of a Savior. When we succeed and they're thankful, we feel fantastic! But when we fail, or they think we've failed, we feel almost as depressed as Peter after he denied Christ.

Some of us vacillate between the two extremes, living for smiles but dreading a frown. The compulsion to fix others' problems is driven by fear of not being accepted. The fear isn't limited to our role as trusted friends. If we struggle with these issues of identity and overresponsibility, we struggle with it in every aspect of our lives. Let me be painfully honest about this crucial issue.

Each of us can learn to take responsibility to communicate clearly and appropriately with others. We can set boundaries that protect us and still allow us to have good, healthy relationships—a blend of independence and intimacy. A living cell can illustrate healthy boundaries. In our bodies the cell walls are semipermeable membranes that serve to keep poisons out, let nutrients in, excrete waste, and define the existence of the cell as separate and distinct from others.

Relational boundaries do the same things. They enable us to stop others from poisoning our lives with their abuse and criticism. They encourage us to develop affirming relationships. By staying away from poisonous people, we are then able to grieve the losses we have experienced so we can experience healing. We develop the wonderful ability to be the people God wants us to be—independent, but intimate with Him and with trustworthy people.

These statements characterize good boundaries. Check those that you consider characteristic of you.

- ❑ "This is what I will do. That is what I won't do."
- ❑ "I will not allow this kind of behavior anymore."
- ❑ "I'm not responsible for his or her happiness or success."
- ❑ "I refuse to be manipulated."
- ❑ "I'm sorry. I wish I could help you, but I can't."
- ❑ "Here's how I feel when you do/say that."
- ❑ "I don't want to talk about this right now."
- ❑ "I want to talk about this right now."

Another tool in setting good boundaries is a simple set of statements: "I feel … I want … I will …" In a difficult situation, you can say, "I feel hurt when you treat me like this. I want to have a loving, respectful relationship. I will treat you with respect, and that means calling attention to your cursing and your anger when you are out of control." Of course, if the person becomes belligerent when you use these statements, skip over the "I feel" part and go to the other two. Don't give him any ammunition, such as your own feelings, to use against you!

Those of us who compulsively rescue others from their problems can learn to listen patiently and then, like Jesus with the crippled man at the pool, we can ask, "What can I do to help you?" Instead of jumping in and doing too much for people, we can be more objective and help them take their own steps of progress. If we have been rescuing them, it is best to back away and let that person learn to take responsibility.

When we stop fixing others' problems, we might hear the accusation, "You're being so selfish!" That's the worst thing a compulsive fixer can hear! But stay strong and don't give in. Changing the patterns of our lives and relationships requires courage and tenacity, but it also requires consistency to convince others that we won't give in if they continue to whine. We have to train ourselves to act differently, and we need to train others too. If we are consistent, sooner or later they will realize that no amount of whining, complaining, or accusing will make us go back to our old compulsive ways. We have changed!

We need to realize that a lack of boundaries is harmful not only for us but for others in our lives too. It has kept them from being responsible, facing the truth about themselves, and taking necessary action. The best thing we can do for them, then, is to set good boundaries and stick to them. They may not like it at first, but after some adjustments, everyone will be much better off for it.

When we begin to set boundaries with people—either those who have hurt us or those we try to help—we often feel tremendous guilt and confusion. When others condemn us for being selfish or they don't understand why we want them to make their own decisions, we are tempted to cave in and go back to the old ways.

Setting boundaries—and sticking with them—illustrates being obedient to God to live according to our strong, new identity in Christ, and it sustains and nurtures that new identity. In addition, our honesty and strength is the best role model for others. Our willingness to speak the truth and set boundaries creates an environment of integrity, and it gives others an opportunity to be responsible. That's the role of a trusted friend.

Where are you in terms of a good balance between compassion and healthy boundaries?

COMPASSION RULES ME.   I KNOW MY BOUNDARIES.

Imagine yourself as having a strong sense of identity, the ability to think clearly, genuine compassion for hurting people, and the capacity to set strong, healthy boundaries.

Which of these characteristics describe you? Underline them.

Which of these characteristics do you need to develop? Circle them.

SOME DIFFICULT ISSUES

Many Christians (especially women) are confused about setting boundaries because they are told they have to be obedient and submit, even to abusive people. Various passages of Scripture are used to back up this instruction, and the boundaryless person feels obligated to go along—but furious at feeling controlled. We need a broader perspective on this issue, one that takes the full teaching of Scripture into account. Let's look at three principles:

The right of self-protection

Some Bible teachers say that a Christian has no rights at all. In one sense, that is true. If we call Christ "Lord," we submit ourselves to His leading, wherever, whenever, and however He may direct us. We have no rights to go against the will of God, but He has given us the right, the authority, and the responsibility to act appropriately in human relationships.

As His beloved children, we are to be strong and wise. Jesus admonished us to be "wise as serpents, and harmless as doves" (Matt. 10:16, KJV). That means we are to understand the dynamics of motives and actions in relationships, but act with astute wisdom, not in manipulation or revenge. When someone is abusing or controlling us, we are to protect ourselves. Paul warned Timothy about a man who had attacked him: "Alexander the metalworker did me a great deal of harm. The Lord will repay him for what he has done. You too should be on your guard against him, because he strongly opposed our message" (2 Tim. 4:14-15).

In the same way, we need to be on guard against those who have hurt us or who threaten to hurt us. Being on guard, however, doesn't mean we counterattack. Paul's encouragement to Timothy was the assurance that God Himself would repay Alexander for hurting him. It is entirely appropriate for us to protect ourselves, but not to take revenge.

The nature of love

We are to submit first and foremost to the Lord, not to people. We are to obey Him at all cost and at all times. The question then is: What is the Lord's will in a difficult situation? We find many passages in the Bible that instruct us to "love one another," but many of us are confused about what it means to love an addict or an abusive person.

If an alcoholic asked you for a drink, would it be loving to give him a bottle? No, of course not. Giving him alcohol may be submissive to his will, but it wouldn't be in his best interests; therefore, it wouldn't be honoring to the Lord. In the same way, if a demanding, abusive, manipulative person commands you to submit, is it loving to give in? No.

The loving thing is to confront his behavior and help him take steps toward self-control, responsibility, and kindness.

Submitting out of fear may be obeying that person, but it isn't obeying God—and it isn't loving that person because it isn't what is best for him. Paul wrote the Romans: "Love must be without hypocrisy" (Rom. 12:9, HCSB). We are hypocrites if we cower in fear, obey an abusive person, and then call it love. Genuine love is strong enough to speak the truth and do what is best for someone else, even if he doesn't like it. Genuine love also seeks wisdom to make sure we are doing the right thing, not becoming a doormat or compulsively fixing because we are afraid, and conversely, not refusing to help because we are angry.

Read Ephesians 4:14-16. What is the meaning of "speaking the truth in love"?

Responding to a fool

Another set of passages that can be applied to setting boundaries is found in the Book of Proverbs. Many of the proverbs talk about wisdom and foolishness. A "fool" is someone who is stubborn and demands his own way, even when that hurts other people and himself. Here is a small sample of passages:

"Fools mock at making amends for sin, but goodwill is found among the upright" (14:9). Foolish people won't admit they are wrong.

"A fool finds no pleasure in understanding, but delights in airing his own opinions" (18:2). Foolish people don't listen to others, but they insist that we listen to them.

"A fool gives full vent to his anger, but a wise man keeps himself under control" (29:11). Foolish people sometimes explode in rage and use their anger to intimidate others. Foolish people say things that hurt others instead of healing them.

How should we respond to foolish people? There are times when we need to be silent and not get into an argument with a foolish person, but there are other times when we need to speak boldly to refute him. It takes wisdom to know the difference.

"He who walks with the wise grows wise, but a companion of fools suffers harm" (13:20). If we spend too much time around foolish people, we inevitably will be hurt. But if we choose to spend time with loving, kind, wise people, we will become like them.

Are we to forgive those who have hurt us and who continue to try to control us? Yes, we are commanded by God to forgive them. Should we trust them? Forgiveness and trust are separate issues. We are commanded to forgive, but we are never commanded to trust. Trust must be earned by kind, respectful, consistent behavior. Trusting those who haven't proven they are trustworthy is especially foolish.

CARING FOR GOD'S FLOCK

The memory verse at the beginning of week 5 identifies the role of shepherds in caring for hurting people. Throughout history, shepherds have led their flocks to pasture and water, and they have protected them from wolves. When any of the sheep wandered off, shepherds searched for them until they found them and brought them back safe and sound. Christ is the ultimate shepherd, and He has given us the privilege of working with Him to care for others.

In today's Christian environment, people can wander into and out of church life with few people noticing. Those who are missing are especially vulnerable if they haven't connected with people in a Sunday School class, a Bible study or small group, or in a service group. Pastors can't care for all the sheep by themselves. They need caring people who connect with newcomers, build strong relationships with members and regular attenders, and communicate with them when they are in need.

For a variety of reasons, hurting people often don't connect with anyone at the church, so they "fall through the cracks." One of the responsibilities and privileges of trusted friends is to be the eyes and ears of the church family to notice people who may need help but who may quickly fall away if nobody reaches out to them. Be a good shepherd to these sheep. Start a conversation, make a connection, lend a listening ear, and point people in a direction that meets their needs. But even if you refer them to a class or group in the church or to an agency in the community, stay in touch. In this way, your church will be known by your love (John 17:23,26).

Read John 10:14-16. Pray and thank God for being a wise Shepherd.

---

1. Gary R. Collins. *Christian Counseling: A Comprehensive Guide.* Copyright © 1988 Gary R. Collins, p. 105.

week six

GETTING STARTED

"**Whatever you do,** work at it with all your heart, as working for the Lord, not for men, since you know that you will receive an inheritance from the Lord as a reward."
Colossians 3:23-24

This week we'll look at a number of situations in which people need a trusted friend. These case studies give you the opportunity to imagine yourself in these relationships, and consider how to help each of these people. You will have the benefit of your small group members to offer insights and evaluation.

CASE STUDIES

For each case study think about people you've known in similar situations and imagine helping them. For our purposes jot down your thoughts and plans for each of three conversations, and use this template for your planning (though in some cases, you won't need all three):

First meeting—Goal: to establish trust and begin to uncover the real needs.

When and where will you meet with this person, couple, or family?

What questions can help uncover their thoughts and feelings?

What are come complicating factors that might be important to discover (such as tension in the family, family of origin problems, sibling rivalry, health problems, debt, etc.)?

How will you determine if, how, and when you will share Scripture and prayer with them?

What do you hope to accomplish in this first conversation?

Second meeting—Goal: to clarify the real needs of the person.

What listening skills would be good to use to validate feelings and uncover real hurts and hopes?

How will you discern the real needs of each person involved?

How will you communicate your insights about what they need next?

Would it be good to invite another person to the next meeting? Why or why not?

How will you determine what Scriptures to share and when to pray with them?

What do you hope to accomplish in this second conversation?

Third meeting—Goal: to make a good referral and help the person make that connection successfully.

What are some possible resources to recommend?

How will you paint a picture of hope and health for this family?

What does the couple need in order to contact the resources and actually get substantive help?

How can you and the church provide ongoing support?

Case Study #1

A couple is distraught because their 15-year-old daughter is spending most of her time with a 19-year-old young man, and they suspect their daughter is sexually active. She seems to be completely preoccupied with this young man, whom they don't trust at all. She often comes home late on weekends, and she's furious when her parents try to discipline her.

First meeting:

Second meeting:

Third meeting:

Case Study #2

The husband of a lady in your Sunday School class died yesterday of a heart attack. He was 53. Her children live out of state and can't be with her until tomorrow.

What will you do to provide comfort and care for her today, tomorrow, and in the coming weeks?

Today:

Tomorrow:

Ongoing support:

Case Study #3

A young couple is experiencing tremendous tension in their relationship. They each have promising careers, but the wife wants to have a baby. They are deep in debt because they bought a house that was too big, cars that were too expensive, and the finest clothes they could buy. Now they are experiencing conflict because both have to keep working to pay the bills so they can maintain their standard of living. For several weeks you notice that she's unhappy, so after church you find her alone and ask if she wants to talk. She begins to cry and spill all her pain of not being understood by her husband and feeling trapped in the vice of debt and work.

Initial conversation:
Where is the best place and when is the best time to talk with her?

First meeting:

Second meeting:

Third meeting:

Case Study #4

A man who sits near you each Sunday is normally cheerful, but today he seems very unhappy. You ask him if you can help in any way, and he begins to cry. He tells you that his son, recently back from college, has just learned that he has stage 4 cancer.

What will you do at that moment?

How can you provide comfort and care in the next few days?

What resources are available for the man and his son as they deal with their grief, the medical problems, and possibly death? (List referral sources from your directory.)

Case Study #5

A woman confides in you that she is struggling in her marriage. Her husband is a good provider, but he is emotionally distant from her and their three children, ages 18, 15, and 11. When she tries to connect with him more deeply, he withdraws in anger and insists that he's doing the best he can do. In the past couple of months, she has been gaining weight, and she seems depressed.

First meeting:

Second meeting:

Third meeting:

Case Study #6

A couple tells you that their 20-year-old son has been acting strangely for the past year. Sometimes he's extremely energetic and creative. At those times, he barely sleeps because his mind is racing. But at other times he is lethargic and depressed. They don't know what to do.

First meeting:

Second meeting:

Third meeting:

Case Study #7

A good friend of yours has been serving God and the church faithfully, but he's getting burned out. You've suggested he take a break for a few months, but he insists that he can't find anybody to take his place, and besides, he's "just fine." As the weeks and months go by, you notice that he's becoming more critical, and his temper is quite short.

Since he doesn't accept your advice, how should you approach him to win his trust?

How would you uncover the underlying cause of his compulsion to serve?

How would you get into the three conversations with him?

ARE YOU READY?

From the beginning of this training, we saw that a trusted friend is someone who is growing in spiritual and emotional maturity, has the desire to help hurting people, and has time to care for others. Our privilege and responsibility is to listen carefully to others to uncover their hurts and needs, share meaningful passages of Scripture, pray, and refer them to excellent resources. Certainly some of us are more gifted in this effort than others, but all of us are to imitate Christ's love for people.

Throughout the Gospels we see Jesus patiently and intentionally connect with prostitutes, lepers, the sick, crippled, people who were demon-possessed, noisy children, and people from all walks of life. In each of these He gave undivided attention, genuine love, and the resources of His grace, forgiveness, and power. As we follow Him, that's what we'll do too.

Some may be wondering, *How will people find me? How will people in the church or in the community contact me so I can help them?* Those are excellent questions. As God uses us to help hurting people, the word will spread that we can be trusted, that we truly care, and that God has allowed us to be part of His plan to change people's lives. A good reputation is a wonderful calling card, and we can be sure that others will seek out people who are known for their love, honesty, and strength.

At times God will send people to us seemingly out of nowhere. We'll be like Philip, who found himself sharing Christ with the Ethiopian eunuch in the back of a chariot on a hot dusty road in Palestine. (See Acts 8:26-39.) God will sovereignly and graciously put hurting people in our paths so we can help them.

In what ways has God qualified you to be a trusted friend?

In what areas do you need to grow a bit more?

COMPLETING REFERRAL SOURCES

Last week we discussed a number of possible referral resources. As we conclude our study, we need to identify those that have earned and continue to earn our confidence. At this point take some time to finalize your list.

• Look for any gaps that need to be filled. For instance, if you need to find an adolescent counselor, call a local counselor you trust for a recommendation. If you need to find a drug and alcohol rehab facility, contact a counselor or support group facilitator for a referral. Or if you need a women's shelter, call a community "hot line," the police department, or the staff of another organization for information.

• Prioritize the referral sources on your list. Not all agencies, attorneys, support groups, or counselors are equally skilled or knowledgeable to meet a particular need. People you refer count on you to send them to the best sources of help, so do your homework to find out as much as possible about the ones on your list.

• Continue to fine-tune your list. As you refer people and get feedback, you may find that some of those on your list give outstanding care, but others aren't as helpful. Don't jump to conclusions—several different factors can lead to a negative report—but look for patterns in the feedback and adjust your recommendations accordingly.

Look over the list from Week 5. Look for gaps, prioritize those in each category, and, as much as possible, complete your referral list. Keep the list with you or in an accessible place so you'll have the information you need.

LIMITATIONS

All of us have limitations. One of these is time. We simply don't have enough hours in the day and enough compassion in our emotional tanks to care for everybody. Even Jesus spent time alone to recharge, refresh, and rekindle His sense of purpose and His intimacy with the Father so He could keep going strong. If He recognized His limitations, we should recognize ours far more!

Another limitation is our field of expertise. God has given each of us experiences that have challenged us and equipped us to help others. Some of us feel completely comfortable helping families of those who struggle with mental illness, some enjoy helping people addicted to drugs, some are skilled in helping couples with troubled marriages, and some are especially gifted to comfort people at the bedside or graveside.

As God uses you to care for people, you'll find that He uses you more powerfully—and you have more joy in your efforts—as you help people with needs similar to those you have experienced. That's not a flaw; it's a gift. Use it with joy and tailor your efforts to help people with those needs as much as possible.

Be careful to follow wise and rational guidelines. As a rule, men shouldn't meet with women, except perhaps in a public place for one conversation. And men shouldn't meet with teenage girls anytime unless the men's wives or another adult woman accompanies them.

All of us need feedback and advice from time to time. If we try to be Lone Rangers out there caring for people, we'll make mistakes, hurt others, and become exhausted. Each of us needs at least one person we can go to from time to time for encouragement and answers to tough questions. For you, this person may be your pastor, department director, class teacher, women's or men's ministry leader, small group leader, a professional counselor in your community, or someone else you trust and who has time to assist you.

What are your areas of experience in helping people?

Who is that one person you can count on for help as you try to help needy people?

Which of these could be effective in helping a hurting person?
Check all that apply.

- ❏ a mechanic
- ❏ a government employee
- ❏ a florist
- ❏ a store owner or employee
- ❏ a real estate agent
- ❏ a used car salesman

How could you help others through your job?

GO AND OVERFLOW

John told his readers that we can love others because we've experienced the transforming warmth of God's love (1 John 4:11). Paul reminded people that we can forgive because we've been forgiven (Col. 3:13) and accept people because God has accepted us by His grace (Rom. 15:7). Love, forgiveness, and acceptance of others, then, overflows from our "innermost beings" into the lives of others as we experience God's grace and strength.

But we can't give away something we don't possess. If we've experienced God's comfort in times of pain, we can share that comfort with others. Paul reminded the Corinthians that God "comforts us in all our troubles, so that we can comfort those in any trouble with the comfort we ourselves have received from God" (2 Cor. 1:4). If we've learned lessons about standing strong when everything in us wants to wilt, we can help others stand up too. If we've been flooded with the love of God when all we felt was shame, we can show compassion to those who despise themselves. And if we've survived times of darkness by clinging to the truth of God even though our emotions told us to run from Him, we can give hope to people in their darkest moments.

For the love, truth, and strength of God to flow from us to others, it has to be real in our own hearts. If it isn't real, our efforts will be designed to win approval and fill the hole in our hearts. But if God has worked His grace and purposes deep into our souls, we'll overflow with His kindness in our relationships with hurting people. That's our responsibility as trusted friends. And that's our great privilege.

What are the most important things you've learned from this training about:

the needs of others

the skills needed to be a trusted friend

your motive for helping people

your limitations

how to rely on the Scriptures and prayer as integral parts
of your efforts

Who are some people you know who need a trusted friend
right now?

Is it appropriate for you to initiate contact with one of them?
❑ yes ❑ no

Take some time to thank God for the experiences He has used to equip you to care for
others, and ask Him for wisdom and guidance to take the next steps to be a more trusted
friend.

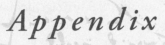

Appendix

Our six weeks of study material limited the amount of content we wanted to include, so we added some important concepts in this appendix. During or after the study take time to review or to read these articles. We trust they will give you additional insight and equip you to be an even more effective trusted friend. We have indicated to which week's content each article refers.

The topics in this appendix include:

- Traditions of Christian Care (week 1) 120
- Stages of Grief (weeks 2 and 3) 122
- Passages of Encouragement and Hope (week 4) 128
- Why People Struggle and Suffer (week 5) 130
- Critical or Chronic Illness (week 5) 134
- The Limits of Confidentiality (week 6) 139

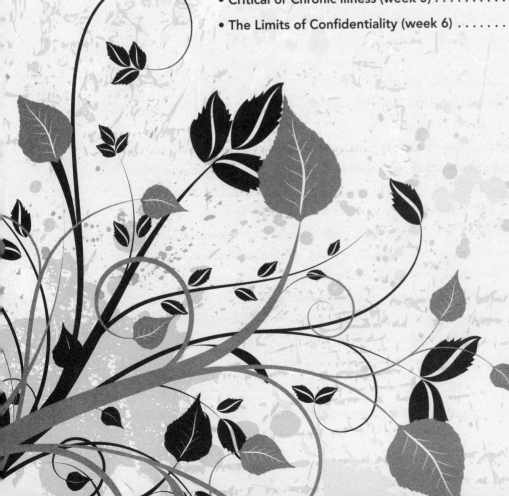

TRADITIONS OF CHRISTIAN CARE

Being a trusted friend is a time-honored role in the history of the church. Since the days Jesus walked on the earth, those who have followed Him have realized that we are called to care for "the least of these." A strong tradition in our spiritual heritage demonstrates genuine love for the unlovely and care for those in need.

In the history of the church, many people may assume that Christian counseling a recent development, but as we look back into our rich history, we find a group of believers who were, perhaps, the strongest Christian counselors the church has ever known. In the 17th and 18th centuries, pastors such as Richard Baxter and Jonathan Edwards were known as "physicians of the soul." Baxter's sermon on depression reveals a clear understanding of the complexity of the emotional, relational, spiritual, and physiological factors in depressed people.

Today we often misunderstand and malign the Puritans. However, Baxter and his fellow Puritans communicated with insight and biblical applications the issues commonly addressed in counseling today. In his book, *Power Religion,* author David Powlison observed:

"The Puritans developed a massive and profound literature on a wide range of personal and pastoral problems. They wrote numerous, detailed case studies. They had a sophisticated diagnostic system that penetrated motives. They had a well-developed view of the long-term processes, the tensions, the difficulties, and the struggles of the Christian life.

"[The Puritans] carefully addressed what the 20th century would term addictions to sex, food, and alcohol; the gamut of problems in marriage and family relationships; depression, anxiety, and anger; perfectionism and the drive to please other people; interpersonal conflict; priorities and management of time and money; unbelief and deviant value systems."[1]

In *The Journal of Pastoral Practice,* Timothy Keller compared and contrasted the counseling habits of the Puritans. He noted that

". . . if Puritans observed Christian counselors today, they "would find many biblical counselors are being far too superficial in their treatment of problems by merely calling for surface repentance and behavioral change. But they also would be quite uncomfortable with the 'inner healing' approaches which virtually ignore behavior. . Above all, the Puritans' 'spirit' would differ quite a bit from other counselors today. Most modern evangelical counselors simply lack the firmness, directness and urgency of the Puritans. Most of us talk less about sin than did our forefathers. But, on the other hand, the Puritans were amazingly tender, encouraging, always calling the counselees to accept the grace of God and extremely careful not to call a problem 'sin' unless it was analyzed carefully. One of their favorite texts was: 'A bruised reed he will not break, and a smoking flax he will not quench.' "[2]

Many different models of counseling—and almost as many models in Christian counseling—have changed through the years. Genuinely Christ-centered care, though, contains some common, important elements:

appendix

- It acknowledges the legitimate expression of emotions in the process of uncovering hidden perceptions and wounds and in the resolution and healing of those wounds.
- It acknowledges that many of the problems people experience result from attempts to meet genuine needs in ways apart from God's design.
- It acknowledges that Christ-centered counseling can only be provided by a person whose faith in Christ provides empathy, love, insight, and direction.
- It acknowledges that the truth of Scripture is the first and foremost source of wisdom and insight about the human condition, needs, and remedies.
- It acknowledges the need to carefully observe each person's situation to see how the Scriptures can be applied most specifically and powerfully.
- It acknowledges the importance of a powerful blend of God's work and our responsibility, of the Holy Spirit's power, and the role of spiritual disciplines.

As you serve in the role of a trusted friend, realize that your care for people is in the tradition of countless others who trusted Christ to use them in tender and powerful ways to transform the lives of hurting, needy people.

Does knowing you serve in a long tradition of Christian care give you insight and encouragement? ❑ yes ❑ no

Does it change how you think about the care you provide? If so, how?

121

STAGES OF GRIEF

Many Christians don't know how to grieve, and they don't allow others to take steps through the grieving process. Sadly, many Christians give dumb and hurtful answers to people who have suffered loss. In his book *Treasures from the Dark,* Dr. Ike Reighard recalls that when his wife and baby died in childbirth, one well-meaning person tried to comfort him by saying, "It'll be all right." He thought, *No, it won't be all right. They're dead.* And another person compared Ike's tragic loss with the pain she felt when her dog died. (Yes, she actually said that to him a few hours after the deaths.).

For examples, read what happened to these individuals when they attempted to share their grief with Christian friends.

1. The board meeting dragged on for a while, but before they left, the chairman asked if anyone had any prayer requests. Phil's voice broke as he explained, "You probably know that my wife Jan had a miscarriage four weeks ago. We're still pretty shaken up by it. Would you pray for us?"

As soon as Phil finished asking for prayer, Stan turned to him and asked, "Brother, that was four weeks ago. It's time you put that behind you and go on with your life."

2. Two months after Margaret's teenage daughter was killed in a car wreck, she returned to her Bible study group. That first week her emotions were raw. She sat in a daze through most of the meeting, but toward the end, she began to weep uncontrollably.

The group stopped to focus on Margaret's pain. Several women patted her on the back and shoulders; then Rachel told her, "Honey, you know God doesn't want you to hurt like this. You need to give it all to Him and let Him take the pain away."

3. John and Betty stood where their living room used to be. A hurricane had devastated their community, and now, weeks later, they looked for any semblance of keepsakes they had cherished. John found a frame with a water-stained photograph of them with their three children from 20 years ago when the kids were young Betty picked up the tattered remnants of a quilt her grandmother had given her on their wedding day.

A man helping with clean-up wanted to give them perspective. He walked over to them and declared, "You know, all this was going to burn anyway. You can't take it with you. It's only stuff."

Select one of these stories and describe how you think the hurting person might have responded.

What would have been an appropriate way for a trusted friend to have responded to the situation?

Years ago, Elisabeth Kubler-Ross described the reactions of terminally ill cancer patients to their disease. Her book, *On Death and Dying*, described five stages of grief for these patients: denial, anger, bargaining, depression, and acceptance. Soon counselors recognized that these stages of grief apply to any significant loss, not just disease and death.

Many of the people we encounter at church have experienced genuine, painful loss. Some experience the loss of a mate or children, but others suffer grief just as real, such as the loss of feeling safe and loved by parents, the loss of affection and respect from a spouse, the loss of self-respect, the loss of a job. Some grieve the inability to provide financially due to a chronic illness, the loss of close friends and family who move to another community, or the loss of personal faculties because of aging. Indeed, virtually all the problems we face create, to one degree or another, a sense of loss.

appendix

As we become trusted friends to those around us, we need to grasp these stages so we—and those we are trying to help—aren't surprised by intense emotions and seemingly odd behavior. The stages aren't mechanical. A person may move quickly through one phase and then slowly through another. Or someone may drift back and forth between two stages for a while. Generally, however, we don't move to another stage until and unless we have dealt adequately with the previous one.

Many Christians aren't comfortable with processes, especially painful ones. Our instant society and our desire for God to work quickly create expectations that "it just shouldn't be this hard or this slow" to get over a major loss. But it is this hard, and it is this slow. If we feel uncomfortable with the process of grieving losses (maybe because we need to grieve a loss that has gotten postponed), we will give quick, superficial answers to questions that demand insight and patience. And we will block the grieving process instead of facilitating it.

Do you agree or disagree with the statement that "many Christians aren't comfortable" with the process of grief? Explain your answer.

Let's examine these stages:

1. Denial

The first and instinctive reaction to bad news—especially, traumatic news—is to insist the news isn't true.

"That can't be!" Bob told his doctor who broke the news about his pancreatic cancer.

Marie's counselor gently coaxed her to talk about the emotional abuse she endured from her mother, but she immediately slammed her emotional door shut. She shook her head, "But it didn't bother me. I'm strong. Those words didn't hurt me at all."

What are some words you would use to characterize this stage?

Read 2 Samuel 12:15-17. Describe how David grieved over his son's sickness.

Eventually the person will come to grips with the loss and move into the second stage of grief.

2. Anger

Loss isn't theoretical; it's personal. And like Adam in the garden, we look for someone to blame, someone on whom we focus our anger.

Susanne lashed out at her husband about their son's tragic death. She shrieked, "Why did you let him drive the car that night? He's dead! Do you know that? He's dead!"

Dustin seethed as he recounted beatings he took from his father. "He always used a belt, and he knew how to use it."

What are some experiences that might move someone out of denial to anger?

Anger doesn't last too long, however. If it isn't resolved, it turns to bitterness. Author and pastor Frederick Buechner observed: "Of the Seven Deadly Sins, anger is possibly the most fun. To lick your wounds, to smack your lips over grievances long past, to roll over your tongue the prospect of bitter confrontations still to come, to savor to the last tooth some morsel of both the pain you are given and the pain you are giving back—in many ways it is a feast fit for a king. The chief drawback is that what you are wolfing down is yourself. The skeleton at the feast is you!"[3]

Many people never move out of this stage of grief. Bitterness becomes their constant companion, and the desire for revenge consumes the rest of their lives.

What are some characteristics of this stage?

appendix

Read Hebrews 12:15. Describe what happens when we allow anger to fester?

3. Bargaining

If sufferers can find appropriate resolution for their anger, they usually move into another difficult stage: bargaining.

Beth recounted her childhood in an alcoholic home. "My father was absent most of the time," she remembered, "and when he was home, he was hung over. My mother's life revolved around my dad and my brother. Both of them were always into trouble. I've been going to counseling for a while now, but the one question I want answered is: What can I do to get my mother to love me? That's all I really want."

In this stage people want to swap something they have for something they desperately want. Quite often the bargain makes no sense at all. It can seem like trusting in magic or superstition.

Beth kept doing exactly what she'd been doing her whole life: whatever she thought would make her mother happy. Her new realization of the pain caused by her home life wasn't yet coupled with an understanding that she couldn't make her mother responsible, loving, and good.

A grieving mother decided to go to church every day at a particular time in the hope that God would heal her son who had been stricken with MS.

A man stopped cursing and expected a great job to land in his lap.

Bargaining is especially harmful because it's based on a strong hope that God or another person will finally come through. And hope is a good thing, isn't it? But bargaining is a "hopeless hope" based on magic, not truth; on manipulation, not personal responsibility. Many people never move beyond this stage of grief because they know that when they give up their hopeless hope, they'll feel utterly, completely empty.

Read Genesis 18:23-32. What bargain did Abraham try to make with God?

4. Depression

This stage could be called "sadness" because of the profound sense of the reality of the loss. No denials, no reactions of anger, and no attempts to swap something to gain love and life.

Now, the person with end-stage cancer is overwhelmed with the reality of impending death. The sexually abused woman comes to grips with the devastation she has endured. The parent of a chronically sick child realizes that he will never get well. And the crushing weight of reality is almost more than anyone can bear.

What are some factors that would cause someone to move beyond bargaining to depression?

In your opinion how serious is the state of depression?

❏ It's largely exaggerated and a bid for attention.
❏ Christians should learn to put the past in the past.
❏ Depression is a cry for help.
❏ Other _____

Depressed people rarely find the way out of their gloom without intervention through medicines and/or counseling. The stage of depression and sadness isn't comfortable for us, but it is a necessary step of processing loss.

Read Jonah 3. His anger became depression as he prayed to die.
Was he handling depression appropriately? (circle)   Yes   No
What did God do to relieve his depression?

5. Acceptance

After a time of tears and sadness, the well of hopelessness is drained dry, and people realize they still have something to live for. Even if that life is only days or weeks long, the person can still share love and impart a legacy of hope.

Those whose grief comes from relational trauma surface from their sadness and realize they can still trust God to give them a meaningful, wonderful, and joyous life. No, life isn't what they hoped it would be, but they can make the most of the friendships, health, and purpose they've found. God didn't make the pain go away, and He didn't fix all the problems. But He is kind and loving. He is powerful and present. His ways are not like our ways, but we can be confident that even if nothing in our lives makes sense, He is near and we can trust Him.

> Describe the insights and wisdom a person in this stage probably
> has gained from the grueling process of grief.

Many experts have concluded that it takes two years to grieve a significant loss, three years for an accidental death in the family, and four years for violent deaths of loved ones. "Significant losses" also include strained and broken relationships, addictions and compulsive disorders, living with those with these problems, loss of a job, and a host of similar difficulties. And these periods of time are valid only if the person is actively pursuing the grieving process by being honest about emotions, gaining insight, and experiencing the support of friends.

Those who don't pursue this process with tenacity and patience find themselves blocked in one of the earlier stages. Quite often a crisis (like a panic attack or an angry response to a relatively minor problem) shakes up our lives and reminds us that we still have steps we need to take in dealing with loss.

As you meet people who need a friend, realize that almost every one of them is experiencing significant loss. Anticipate the inherent attitudes and behaviors in each stage so you aren't caught off guard. At the right time, share insights you've learned about the process of grieving.

> If you or a friend has suffered significant loss in the recent past,
> describe the loss.

> For you or your friend, identify the stage of grief now being
> experienced.

> What are some ways people can know they are actively processing
> their grief in order to move to the next stage?

PASSAGES OF ENCOURAGEMENT AND HOPE

Anxiety
Psalms 34:4-7; 46:1-3,7; Proverbs 3:24-26; Luke 12: 6-7,22-31;
Philippians 4:6-8; 1 Peter 5:6-7

Anger
Psalms 4:4; 103:8-12; Proverbs 15:1; 16:32; 103:8-12; Matthew 5:22;
Romans 12:19-21; Ephesians 4:25-32

Death
Psalm 116:15; John 5:24-29; 1 Corinthians 15:51-58;
2 Corinthians 1:3-4; Hebrews 2:14-18; 9:27; 1 John 5:11-13

Debt
Psalms 37:21; 25:21-26; Proverbs 22:7; Matthew 18:23-34;
Romans 13:8

Depression
Psalms 27:13-14,34; 103:1-8; Proverbs 15:13; John 16:24;
Romans 15:13; Philippians 4:6-9; Colossians 3:15-16; 1 Peter 5:7

Fear
Psalms 18:1-3; 27:1-3; 34:4-7,15-18; 91; Proverbs 1:33; 3:24-26;
Luke 12:5; Romans 8:15; 2 Timothy 1:7; Hebrews 13:6; 1 John 4:18

Forgiveness
Psalms 32:1-2; 85:2; 86:5; 103:1-3,12; Matthew 6:12-15; 18:21-22;
Mark 11:25; Luke 17:3-4; 2 Corinthians 5:17-18; Ephesians 1:6-7;
4:31-32; Colossians 2:13-14; 3:13; Hebrews 8:12; 1 John 1:9; 2:1-2

Grief

Psalms 23:4; 119:50; Matthew 5:4; 1 Corinthians 15:55-58;
2 Corinthians 1:2-4; 5:8; 1 Thessalonians 4:13-14;
2 Thessalonians 2:16-17; 1 Peter 5:7; Revelations 21:4

Guilt

Psalms 51:1-4,7-9; 103:11-12; 139:22; Proverbs 21:2-3,8;
Romans 3:23; James 2:8-12; 1 John 1:9

Mercy

Psalms 4:1; 51:1-5,15-17; Lamentations 3:22-23; Matthew 5:7; 9:13;
Luke 1:50; 10:29-37; Ephesians 2:4-6; Titus 3:5; Hebrews 4:16;
James 2:12-13; 3:17

Patience

Psalms 27:14; 37:7-9; 40:1; Romans 8:25; 15:4-5; Galatians 5:22;
1 Thessalonians 5:14; 2 Thessalonians 1:4; 1 Timothy 6:11-12;
Hebrews 6:1-15; 10:35-37; 12:1; James 1:2-4; 5:7-8

Peace

Psalms 34:8,22; 37:37; 59:16-17; 113; 119:165; Proverbs 3:1-4;
Matthew 5:9; John 14:27; 16:33; Romans 5:1; James 3:17

Sorrow/Comfort

Psalms 6:2-9; 51; Matthew 5:4; John 14:1-2; 16:20-22;
2 Corinthians 1:3-7; 7:9-11; 1 Thessalonians 4:13-18

Worry

Psalms 4:8; 27:1-3; 46:1-2; 56:3-4; 118:6; 119:165;
Proverbs 3:5-6; Matthew 6:25-34; 10:19; Mark 13:11; John 14:1;
Romans 8:31; Philippians 4:6-7; Hebrews 13:5-6

WHY PEOPLE STRUGGLE AND SUFFER

Many people mean well, but the "help and advice" they offer is simplistic, and in the end, devastating to the person they are trying to assist. They may say their answer for any problem is, "It's sin, and you need to repent" or "Just pray about it." In some cases they have accurately identified the problem (though perhaps they could have communicated it more graciously), but many times the situation is much more complex and requires more understanding of the causes of human suffering.

What are some shallow, simplistic answers you've heard people give as advice for hurting people?

What impact do you think those statements had on those who heard them?

People experience difficulties in their lives for a host of reasons. Some of these include:

• Personal sin: Before people came to Christ, Paul described them as "powerless," "ungodly," "sinners," and "enemies" of God (Rom. 5:6-10, NIV). And after we trust Christ as our Savior, we continue to struggle against our corrupt "old nature" (Rom. 8:12-14; Eph. 4:22-24; Col. 3:1-10). Until we die and are then transformed into the image of Christ (see Rom. 8:29; 1 Cor. 13:12; 1 John 3:2), we will struggle with our selfish hearts.

• Others' sins: All of us suffer from our own selfish, sinful choices, and all of us suffer from the bad choices others have made. We are wounded by an abusive or distant parent, a drunk driver, or a careless remark by a friend. The pain is deepest, though, when we are hurt by those we trusted the most.

• A fallen world: When the universe was created, God pronounced it "good," but sin affected our planet just as it affected our hearts. Earthquakes, fires, hurricanes, tornadoes, floods, poisonous insects, and a host of other calamities remind us that we "groan" for the redemption of creation (Rom. 8:18-25). Almost every night on the news we realize again that the world is fallen and waiting for God's hand to make things right again.

• Waiting: Throughout the psalms, we read encouragement to "wait on the Lord." But waiting is hard. Pastor Chuck Swindoll has said that waiting is the most difficult thing God asks of us. We live in an instant society with drive-thru windows, online banking, ATMs, and microwave cooking. We expect our all needs—and our wants—to be met immediately. But as we follow Christ, His plan inevitably involves times of waiting.

During those times it seems that He is excruciatingly slow. We are tempted to give up on Him and His promises, but God uses those times of emptiness and darkness to teach us lessons of dependence that we couldn't learn any other way.

• The sovereign plan of God includes suffering: We have a hard time with this one, but the Bible makes it clear that God sometimes orchestrates difficulties and suffering to achieve his divine purposes. Isaiah records God saying:

> *"I form the light and create darkness,*
> *I bring prosperity and create disaster;*
> *I, the LORD, do all these things" (Isa. 45:7).*

This verse doesn't fit neatly into our view of a kind and gentle Heavenly Father, but we have to remember that He is also the sovereign King of the universe whose "ways are higher than [our] ways and [whose] thoughts than [our] thoughts" (Isa. 55:9). A study of the sovereignty of God raises almost as many questions as it answers, but sooner or later, we acknowledge the mystery of God's plan and say with Paul:

> *"Oh the depth of the riches of the wisdom and knowledge of God! How unsearch-*
> *able his judgments, and his paths beyond tracing out!*
> *Who has known the mind of the Lord?*
> *Or who has been his counselor?*
> *Who has ever given to God,*
> *That God should repay him?*
> *For from him and through him and to him are all things.*
> *To him be the glory forever! Amen" (Rom. 11:33-36).*

Before we give a definitive answer for why the person sitting in front of us is suffering, we need to take these potential causes into account. In most instances, a combination of factors contributes to the wounds, strained relationships, and blocked goals. Our view of suffering is one of the most significant elements of our philosophy of care giving. Instead of trying to escape suffering at all costs, people can learn to embrace suffering as a tool to draw him into a deeper experience with God. In this way, suffering is viewed as a classroom, not a prison. This distinction realigns the person's goals and hopes, and produces endurance.

Agree or disagree: All pain is caused by sin.
Explain your answer.

Give some specific, real life examples of suffering caused by:

personal sin:

the sins of others:

living in a fallen world:

the crucible of waiting:

God's sovereign, mysterious plan:

Whatever its source, our pain is often an effective tool in the hands of God. In the midst of incredible suffering, Job reflected, "Shall we accept good from God, and not trouble?" (Job 2:10, NIV) In his book *Reaching for the Invisible God,* Philip Yancey stated: "Gregory of Nicea once called St. Basil's faith 'ambidextrous' because he welcomed pleasures with the right hand and afflictions with the left, convinced both would serve God's design for him."[4]

Similarly, Dan Allender wrote in *The Healing Path:* "If we fail to respond appropriately to the wounds that life and relationships inflict, our pain will be wasted; it will numb us or destroy us. But suffering doesn't have to mangle our hearts and rob us of joy. It can, instead, lead us to life—if we know the path to healing. Healing is not the resolution of our past; it is the use of our past to draw us into deeper relationship with god and his purposes for our lives."[5]

> How would it help people (like you, for instance) to welcome
> "pleasures with the right hand and afflictions with the left,
> convinced both would serve God's design for him" (you)?

In an attempt to give hope, Christians sometimes promise more than God intends to deliver. For example, when most believers read the passage at the end of Isaiah 40, they focus on soaring "on wings like eagles." But the grace and power of God are also shown in providing wisdom and strength for those who "run" and don't "grow weary."

At crucial times in a believer's life—especially for those wrestling with emotional and relational difficulties—God promises that he will keep us from fainting if we have the courage to put one foot in front of the other. This last encouragement certainly isn't as grand and glorious as soaring on eagles wings, but it is in line with encouragements to persevere (as in Rom. 5:3-5). Countless faithful Christians have found God's grace to be sufficient even when he didn't take away their pain.

> What might be the consequences of promising people they will
> "soar like eagles" when God's plan is for them to keep walking
> without fainting?

CRITICAL OR CHRONIC ILLNESS

Virtually every day in the life of a church—no matter how large or small it may be—people experience sudden, traumatic illnesses or the draining effect of chronic sickness. In some ways, we care for each of these in the same way: with genuine compassion and a listening ear. But crises and chronic illnesses require different strategies to provide the care people need.

Critical illness

Car wrecks, heart attacks, accidents at home or at work, and a host of other causes send people to the Emergency Room every day. When we find out someone is critically ill and we want to provide care and comfort, we need to consider these preparations.

1. We can find out as much as possible about the illness or injury before we go so that we aren't shocked by what we see when we walk through the door. In some cases, burns or cuts have disfigured the person, or tubes have been inserted to allow for the flow of air, body fluids, or medicines. If we aren't prepared, we may react inappropriately when we walk through the door and see the patient.

2. We should clarify our purpose in visiting the person. Certainly, we want to demonstrate genuine care. Our motive isn't to get lots of information so we can seem like experts when we share "prayer requests" with others or to earn a merit badge by our service. Visiting the sick is a behind-the-scenes ministry that protects the sick person by limiting the amount of information shared with others.

3. The family members of the hospitalized person may be our primary concern when we visit. In some cases, the one who is injured or ill is unconscious or asleep, so our efforts need to be directed toward comforting the family.

4. We should consider who is the best person to make the visit. In many cases, the sick person and the shocked family members don't want or need a parade of well-meaning visitors. They only want a few close friends, and perhaps a pastor, to visit them. We can call one of the family members to ask who they'd like to come for a visit. Then, based on the response, we can call the one they've requested or if asked, go ourselves.

When we visit someone who is critically injured or ill, we should:

1. Observe the visiting hours posted by the hospital.

2. Knock softly if the door is closed before you enter the room. Or if the door is open, get the attention of a nurse or family member to ask for permission to enter the room.

3. Identify yourself to the sick or injured person if you have any doubt you will be recognized. Remember, some people who are critically sick are disoriented or suffer memory loss.

4. Quickly determine how you can best help the sick person and the family members. In most cases, your primary role will be to express your love, offer a prayer, ask if they need anything, and then leave.

5. Stand or sit in an appropriate place where you can have eye contact with the patient and family members. Be careful not to touch any of the medical equipment. If you feel comfortable, touch the person's hand when you enter, when you pray, or when leaving. Human touch is beneficial when done appropriately during your brief stay in the room.

7. Don't ask too many questions, especially about the person's medical condition. And don't see the sick person or the family as a "captive audience" to preach to. Offer words of kindness.

8. If a family member wants to talk more, offer to talk in the waiting room or down the hall in a more private place. Don't get into a long conversation in the sick person's room.

9. Communicate care, listen well, and leave soon.

Chronic illness

Many people recover from traumatic illnesses and injuries and get back to their normal lives, but for some, those days in ICU eventually become weeks, months, and years in nursing homes, assisted living centers, or homebound care. We often associate chronic illness with the elderly, but children with cancer, young adults who have suffered from accidents, and many others in all age groups may be chronically ill.

As time drags on, many of these people experience growing awareness of isolation and loneliness, discouragement, and uselessness. And again, it's not just the sick person who suffers; family caregivers shoulder an enormous emotional, financial, and physical burden.

As you become aware of people whose illness is chronic, consider these steps:

1. Perhaps the best support you can provide is to give the family caregiver a break. Offer to stay for a couple of hours, a morning, or an afternoon to give that person time to get away, relax, or run some errands.

2. Offer comfort, support, a listening ear, and resources to the caregiver.

3. Enlist others to help provide regular care and breaks for the caregiver.

4. Explore the life experiences of the sick person by asking questions about childhood memories and the most pleasant and exciting periods of life. Many elderly people would love for someone to show interest in their life's experiences. Ask questions about their most cherished relationships.

5. Look for a hobby the sick person enjoys (or perhaps used to enjoy or might now enjoy), and provide the resources and encouragement to be involved in those activities.

6. Try to build a network of care for those who are chronically sick and their families. Perhaps a few friends can work out a schedule for them to spend time each week providing care, a listening ear, a warm hug, and a few laughs for someone who desperately needs these distractions from the grind of each day.

Visiting people who are critically ill or injured is often accompanied by the rush of adrenaline because the event happened so suddenly and dramatically. There's nothing wrong with that fact, but visiting people who suffer chronic illnesses need care too. Taking initiative to step into their lives may not be glamorous and exciting, but it fulfills Jesus command to love, give to, and serve those who have nothing to give us in return. Our efforts warm God's heart.

Guidelines for a Hospital Visit

1. When you approach a room, if the door is closed, knock before you enter.
2. Obey such signs as "No Visitors" or "Isolation." If you have any uncertainty, check at the nurse's station.
3. As you enter, look over the room (inconspicuously) and size up the situation. Watch for circumstances that make your visit an inconvenience.
4. Let the patient take the initiative in shaking hands.
5. Be careful where you position yourself. Watch out for tubes and containers attached to the patient. Seat yourself in a place that will not require the patient to move around to keep eye contact.
6. Remember that the patient's condition is personal.
7. Do not visit when you are ill.
8. Resist the temptation to turn the visit into a conference on medical problems.
9. Identify yourself as you enter the room. Remember that the sick person may be disoriented or have a temporary memory loss.
10. Keep your visit brief.

The following are violations of the above guidelines. In the blank write the number of the guideline that has been violated.

____ A. Dorothy wants to make sure she can report accurately on Michelle's condition tonight at prayer meeting. She asks detailed questions about the doctors, the tests, the medications, other treatments, the causes of the problem, and so forth. She leaves with a full report.

____ B. Rhonda drove 30 miles to visit Amy. They are in the same WMU group. The door is closed and has a "No Visitors" sign on it. Rhonda knows that is just so Amy can rest. Surely Amy would not want her to go back home without first coming in for a visit. Rhonda goes in to visit.

____ C. Luther is proud of his record of visiting every member who goes to the hospital. Kathryn had a baby early yesterday morning. She goes home tomorrow. Surely this little cold should not stand in the way of Luther's untarnished record.

___ D. Jimmy is visiting Barry. He discovers they have a common interest in baseball. After two hours of lively discussion, Jimmy has prayer and leaves.

___ E. Paige has just returned to her room from gall bladder surgery. Every movement hurts. Gordon arrives for a visit. He moves to the bedside, gives a strong handshake, and says, "Hi, Friend."

___ F. Mildred and Ruby visit the hospital together each Tuesday. They are in a hurry today to get to a luncheon for the Young at Heart Club. Mr. Sandlin has been admitted for tests. They find his room, open the door, and walk in. They walk back out red-faced. The doctor was examining Mr. Sandlin.

___ G. Wayne had back surgery. Glenn does not want to appear to be in a hurry, so he just sits down in a chair by the head of Wayne's bed.

___ H. Herbert has been undergoing chemotherapy for a common form of cancer. Chester is a new deacon. He knows he may face this same disease with others in his deacon flock. He spends most of the visit learning all he can about the disease—the symptoms, the prognosis, the treatment options, and so forth.

___ I. Karen stops by to visit Rita. She finds that some of Rita's relatives have come from out of town to visit. Karen sees this as an excellent opportunity to get acquainted with Rita's family, so she stays for a visit.

Well, as far as we can tell, no one introduced himself or herself (#9). That may not always be necessary. Just be sure not to leave the patient guessing who you are. Here are the violations: A-6; B-2; C-7; D-10; E-4; F-1; G-5; H-8; I-3.

Using the guidelines for a hospital visit, write what you would do in each of the following situations:

Your pastor calls and asks you to visit one of his close friends. You have had a low-grade fever but feel up to the visit. What would you do?

The sign on the door says "Immediate Family Only."

Doug asks you to have a seat. You realize he will not be able to see you without straining his head. What would you do?

You have just walked in to visit Edith when the nurse delivers supper.

Each hospital visit will be a little different from the others. You must be flexible. You should follow the basic guidelines, however. (1) Even if you want to please your pastor; do not visit if you are sick. Remember your immune system may be weak also. Protect yourself and others. (2) When the sign on the door tells you to keep out, write a note and leave it at the nurse's desk. The nurse can explain when you might be able to visit. (3) Doug is trying to think of your comfort. Your job is to think more about his. If your sitting down is difficult for him, stand up. If you can sit down and talk comfortably with the patient, he will sense that you came for a relaxed, friendly visit. Sometimes standing communicates, "I only have a little time, so let's get this over with quickly." (4) Yes, this is an inconvenient time to visit. Edith will try to be polite and ask you to stay. Excuse yourself anyway. If you must visit on this trip, spend 30 minutes in the coffee shop and then come back.

THE LIMITS OF CONFIDENTIALITY

Confidentiality is, indeed, a hallmark of the relationship between a trusted friend and a person in need. Only in the acknowledged safety of that relationship will people feel free to be honest about their deepest fears, hurts, and hopes. But there's a limit to confidentiality, and that limit is sometimes difficult to determine.

If someone communicates that he or she is homicidal or suicidal, or if we hear about or suspect abuse of a child, a spouse, or an elder, we are required to report this information to the person in authority above us, such as the director of women's ministries or the small groups pastor. Not every statement of hopelessness, however, is a sign of suicidal thoughts, and not every expression of anger means that abuse has occurred.

In most cases, people who are serious about suicide or homicide have a plan. If your friend can articulate a plan, consider him to be a serious threat and take action immediately to inform the person in authority in your church.

If a person is abusing alcohol, illegal drugs, or prescription drugs, don't just tell the person to "Stop it!" Prolonged use of any chemical creates a physiological as well as a psychological dependence on the substance, and if the person stops using too suddenly, withdrawal symptoms can threaten the person's life.

One of the primary resources every trusted friend needs is a gifted physician (often in family practice or an internist) who can assess these often complicated situations and find the best solutions for the person. Of course, the doctor's care is only part of the recovery process for addicts. They need to attend multiple groups each week, find a sponsor who will help them take the hard steps of progress, and soak up spiritual truths about God's grace, love, and power as they trust Him to change their lives.

An even more difficult situation can arise when we become the trusted friend of an adolescent who tells us about sexual promiscuity, self-mutilation, drug use, or some other self-destructive behavior. Should we tell the parents? If we do, we shatter the trust we've established with the adolescent, but if we don't, we may become unwitting accomplices of their behavior.

Ask the adolescent to be honest with his or her parents. If that plea meets with a steadfast refusal, offer to meet with the adolescent and the parents to serve as a mediator. If the adolescent still refuses, ask for assistance from the youth pastor or pastor. The pastor or youth pastor might meet with you and the adolescent to help bring clarity to the young person's thinking.

Don't let yourself get caught in the middle of a strained relationship between an adolescent and parents or between a husband and a wife. If the situation warrants, tell the person you plan to ask for assistance, and go to the person in authority above you, asking for a confidential meeting to discuss the person's problem.

Refer difficult situations to competent, skilled professionals (doctors, counselors, financial planners, social workers, etc.) as soon as possible, and follow up with the individual or the couple to maintain contact and show you care. Don't judge or prejudge the referral source's handling of the situation. That would prejudice your friend and limit the help your friend gets from that source.

If you are genuinely concerned about the quality of care being received, again go to the person in authority over you. Don't tell your friend that you are concerned about the situation.

As trusted friends, we can't fix every problem and mend every relationship. Our role isn't to control people or be their savior. We can only serve as a friend, speak the truth in love, and get help when we need it. People's lives can be train wrecks of relational, physical, financial, and spiritual problems. Our role is to be a sounding board and to encourage people to take the next step. The hard truth is that some will take those steps, but some won't. We can't—and shouldn't—try to force them to change.

Some have asked about the issue of legal liability for trusted friends. Liability is a factor in formal counseling situations; certainly in professional counseling, and to a lesser degree, in lay counseling ministries. The role of a trusted friend, however, isn't formalized, so liability shouldn't be a factor. If you have any questions about this issue, look at *Law and the Christian Counselor* by George Ohlschlager and Peter Mosgovian.

What will you say and do at the moment someone shares thoughts of suicide?

Say:

Do:

What will be your plan of action (talking to authority, providing resources, etc.)?

How will you follow up with that person?

What will you say and do when or if an adolescent confides in you about sexual promiscuity, self-mutilation, drug use, eating disorder, or some other significant problem?

Say:

Do:

What is your plan of action?

How will you follow up with that person?

How will you handle the almost inevitable anger in the friend who feels you have gone outside the relationship to talk to someone else about his or her problem?

Now that you have thought about a couple of specific case studies, write a clear plan for dealing with these limitations of confidentiality, including who will be a resource to you, how you will handle the situation, and how you will handle the almost inevitable anger in the friend who feels you have betrayed a confidence.

---

1. Michael Scott Horton, ed. *Power Religion.* (Chicago: Moody Press, 1992), 191-218.
2. Timothy Keller. "Puritan Resources for Biblical Counseling," *The Journal of Pastoral Practice,* Vol. IX, No. 3 (Wheaton IL: Crossway Books, 1988), 11-44.
3. Frederick Buechner. *Wishful Thinking* (San Francisco: Harper, 1993), 2.
4. Philip Yancey. *Reaching for the Invisible God* (Grand Rapids, MI: Zondervan, 2000), 69.
5. Dan Allender. *The Healing Path* (Colorado Springs: Water Brook Press, 1999).

THE ABCs OF SALVATION

Some people think a personal relationship with God is something only theologians can comprehend. Actually, God's plan of salvation is simple enough for everyone to understand. Here are the ABCs of salvation.

ADMIT

Admit to God that you are a sinner. All persons need salvation. Each of us has a problem the Bible calls sin. Sin is a refusal to acknowledge God's authority over our lives. Everyone who does not live a life of perfect obedience to the Lord is guilty of sin. "For all have sinned and fall short of the glory of God" (Rom. 3:23). Since none of us is perfect, all of us are sinners (Rom. 3:10-18).

The result of sin is spiritual death (Rom. 6:23). Spiritual death means eternal separation from God. By God's perfect standard we are guilty of sin and therefore subject to the punishment for sin, which is separation from God. Admitting that you are a sinner and separated from God is the first step of repentance, which is turning from sin and self and turning toward God.

BELIEVE

Believe in Jesus Christ as God's Son and receive Jesus' gift of forgiveness from sin. God loves each of us. God offers us salvation. Although we have done nothing to deserve His love and salvation, God wants to save us. In the death of Jesus on the cross, God provided salvation for all who would repent of their sins and believe in Jesus. "For God loved the world in this way: He gave His one and only Son, so that everyone who believes in Him will not perish but have eternal life" (John 3:16).

CONFESS

Confess your faith in Jesus Christ as Savior and Lord to others. After you have received Jesus Christ into your life, share your decision with another person. Tell your pastor or a Christian friend about your decision. Following Christ's example, ask for baptism by immersion in your local church as a public expression of your faith. "If you confess with your mouth, 'Jesus is Lord,' and believe in your heart that God raised Him from the dead, you will be saved. With the heart one believes, resulting in righteousness, and with the mouth one confesses, resulting in salvation" (Rom. 10:9-10).

LEADER GUIDE

In the introduction to this Bible study we noted that God has called us to an incredible partnership with Him to touch the lives of hurting people with His grace, truth, and strength. As the group leader, you have the privilege of equipping men and women for this life-changing work.

In the church we often pray for God to "change people's lives." From our experience we've seen this happen most often and most powerfully when a caring person steps into the life of a hurting person to impart God's grace and truth.

In that Spirit-empowered relationship, God works His miracles to open closed minds, soften hardened hearts, and give clear direction for the next step forward. That's the role of a trusted friend, and the role of the leader is to equip each person to be as effective as possible in this role.

As you prepare for the series and each lesson, consider these points:

ASK GOD TO GUIDE YOU AS YOU LEAD.

The curriculum has plenty of principles, examples, and reflection questions to inspire and challenge people, but don't run the group "on auto pilot." Rely on God to guide you as you prepare each week. Trust Him to remind you of particular moments in your own life when a trusted friend stepped in to comfort, correct, and guide you.

Think of times when God used you to care for others. Share your successes, but also share a few of your failures. People will appreciate your honesty, and they'll be more open about their own fears as they go through the training.

Trust God to work deeply in the lives of the people in your group as they go through these weeks. Each week they will have many opportunities to apply the principles you communicate. Sometimes they'll see great success, but sometimes they'll fail miserably. Ask God for wisdom to use both successes and failures as stepping stones for growth.

ASSIGN HOMEWORK EACH WEEK.

The design of this curriculum requires participants to do some homework each week in preparation for discussions in the group. If they have read the chapter for the week and wrestled with the questions, the discussions will be rich. If some people won't do their homework, don't let that discourage you. Focus on those who have prepared for the group, and gently remind others that they will get much more out of the group if they do their homework.

Week 1 gets off to a flying start, so give group members a book a week before you begin, and ask them to read the content from week 1 and fill in their answers to the questions. Or if you prefer, you can have a meeting to introduce the material a week before you actually begin the curriculum. A session plan is provided in case you prefer an introductory session.

HELP THE GROUP SEE NEEDS AROUND THEM.

To be effective in a caring ministry, we need to be able to see the hurt and stresses that people face so we will be tenderhearted—filled with deep compassion toward others. Some of the people in your group might be prone to jump to conclusions that pain is always the direct result of sin. That may be true in a particular case, but often the cause of trouble is more complicated. Teach people to listen intently and seek to understand.

The Gospel of Mark records a moment when Jesus observed people's needs: "When Jesus landed and saw a large crowd, he had compassion on them, because they were like sheep without a shepherd. So he began teaching them many things" (Mark 6:34).

Most people are skilled at hiding their hurts, so teach people in the group to look beneath the surface behaviors and body language. Anger, compulsive busyness, and church attendance often mask deeply buried fears and hurts that need to come to the surface to be addressed.

KNOW AND OVERFLOW.

Jesus emphatically said, "Apart from me you can do nothing" (John 15:5). Apart from the Spirit's work in us, our efforts to care for others will fail or be selfishly motivated to draw attention to ourselves. The work of being trusted friends puts us in crossroads of people's desperate needs and the opportunity for God to work in their lives. For that reason, heart preparation is critical. As the leader, help people in your group understand the important principle of knowing Christ and letting His Spirit overflow from us (see John 7:37-39).

Remember, we can't express what we don't possess, so we need to focus our hearts on Christ, seek to know Him intimately, and then let His Spirit overflow with love, truth, grace, and power into the lives of needy people. Instruct people in the group to look to Him through the Word, prayer, the guidance of the Holy Spirit, and wise counsel from mature believers. He will lead them as they care for others.

As the leader, rivet your heart on Christ and trust Him to guide you as you lead your group.

Feast on His Word, and lead from the wealth of a heart increasingly overwhelmed with God's goodness and greatness.

DELIVER TRANSFORMATIONAL TRUTH.

Knowledge, humor, skill, and techniques are important in helping others, but Christ and His truth transform hearts. Paul wrote the believers in Rome about the power of truth to change lives: "Therefore, I urge you, brothers, in view of God's mercy, to offer your bodies as living sacrifices, holy and pleasing to God—this is your spiritual act of worship. Do not conform any longer to the pattern of this world, but be transformed by the renewing of your mind. Then you will be able to test and approve what God's will is—his good, pleasing and perfect will" (Rom. 12:1-2).

Truth, however, should never be used as a club to bludgeon someone into submission so he or she accepts a choice we demand. Paul reminded the Ephesian Christians to speak "the truth in love" (Eph. 4:15). As you lead your group, help people grasp the balance of grace and truth, sometimes speaking hard truths with genuine compassion and great patience, and always being true to God's Word.

LOOK FOR HEROES.

Identify those in the group who are already recognized as trusted friends in your church and community. Affirm them, celebrate them, and ask them to share their experiences throughout the curriculum. Those with gifts of compassion don't often rise in leadership, so these people may have been on the sidelines of the church's ministry for years. But now they have a place to shine!

Some of the most gifted trusted friends are quiet people. In the first week or so you may not even hear their voices, but sooner or later you'll hear them share their hearts and experiences. You'll realize what a treasure they are to those who receive their care. Look for these quiet people, and ask them to share their experiences and perspectives. They may be hesitant at first, but they will thrive under your observant, affirming leadership.

EVERYONE CAN BE A TRUSTED FRIEND.

Some people in the group may not have strong relational skills, but they can play an important role in noticing needs and providing resources to meet those needs. They often jump to conclusions too quickly, so teach them to listen well. Their strength may be in research and organization, and they can play a significant role by becoming experts about available resources and referring people to them.

IDENTIFY RESOURCES.

One of the most important roles of a leader in this ministry is to gather information about available, competent resources in the community. First, contact the church office to get information already obtained by the pastoral staff. But don't stop there. Before the group begins, go over the list of possible resources in Week 5 and begin compiling a list. Then, even in the first week of training, ask some people in the group to make some phone calls or visits to assess various agencies, counselors, and other organizations.

One of the most common mistakes caregivers make is forgetting their limitations. We rub shoulders every day with people who have deep, hidden emotional, psychological, and spiritual problems. Those who aren't professionals simply aren't equipped to diagnose and treat problems such as personality disorders, bipolar disorder, and a host of other difficulties people experience. And even many professionals refer to other doctors or psychologists who specialize in treating certain problems.

Compassion for every hurting person is a wonderful gift, but that compassion needs to be tempered and directed by wisdom and the knowledge of good resources for care. Train people in your group to initiate care but to quickly recognize when they are over their heads. Saying, "I don't know, but I'll get some help for you," is the mark of a wise, mature, compassionate person.

Ultimately, the effectiveness of trusted friends rises or falls on two issues: the care we offer and the quality of the professional resources we recommend. For that reason, maintain high standards for the resources you find. Do the necessary homework to assess each one. Ask for references and check with those you have referred to assess the quality of the care they received. Over time you'll be able to add more to your list of resources, and you'll probably decide to delete a few.

EXTENDED CURRICULUM.

Because of time restraints we simply couldn't include everything we wanted to have in this six-week curriculum. The topics in the appendix are important, so become familiar with them, and refer people to particular sections when they need more input on grief, passages of Scripture, limits of confidentiality, and so forth. You may also choose to extend the length of the series to eight or nine weeks to cover the topics in the appendix as you read the specific weeks to which they apply.

MAINTAIN CONFIDENTIALITY IN THE GROUP.

In your group, people will share their own hurts and hopes, so be sure to remind them each week of their commitment to respect confidentiality: "What is said in here stays in here." Nothing will destroy a relationship more quickly than sharing private matters that others have entrusted to us. That's true in our relationships with hurting people in the church and in the community, and it's just as true in the relationships of those being trained to be trusted friends. Solomon reminded us: "A gossip separates close friends" (Prov. 16:28).

Occasionally discussions about wounds, fears, and anger can surface dormant emotions in someone in the group. Instead of being a caregiver, this person needs to receive the care of a trusted friend. This is a delicate situation. The person's needs can dominate the group and absorb the time of training, but you don't want to be callous to the person's obvious hurts. Talk to the person privately, and be a friend. Listen carefully, and find a competent professional to provide the next step of care. Invite the person to continue coming to the group. In most cases, these hurting people will understand the role of the group and the need for outside help. By continuing to attend but not becoming the center of attention, relationships grow stronger and compassion builds in the lives of all the group members.

EXPECT RESULTS.

As you prepare to lead the group each week, come to God with a spirit of expectation. The psalmist assures us,

> "For the LORD God is a sun and shield;
>   the LORD bestows favor and honor;
>   no good thing does he withhold
> from those whose walk is blameless"
> (Ps. 84:11).

You can be sure that equipping men and women to touch the lives of "the least of these" is a "good thing" God will support. In fact, He delights in us when we follow His example to look beyond ourselves to care for those who are hurting. That was Christ's example, and as we follow Him, He'll use us in His process of transforming lives.

But God's magnificent promises are coupled with a warning. The enemy of our souls wants to stop us from imparting the grace of God, and he'll use deception and misunderstanding to cause people to get their eyes off God and on their own grievances. Be aware of both God's incredible purposes and the enemy's schemes to derail your efforts.

Enlist people in the church to pray for you and your group, and be sure to remind those you train that forces are at work that we cannot see: God delights in equipping us and using us, but the enemy wants to stop us so that we don't carry out God's purpose to "heal the brokenhearted." Claim God's promises. Ask Him to work in power and grace, and be aware of anything that gets people's eyes off the Lord during the training process.

Leading a group to become trusted friends provides an awesome opportunity and responsibility. As people in your group learn to offer guidance, love and encouragement, they become God's voice, hands, feet, and heart. Yes, the Lord saves, comforts, and delivers, but in His sovereign, gracious plan, He has chosen to use us as a channel of His message of love and grace to others.

In this work we find an amazing paradox. When we unselfishly give of ourselves as a friend in Jesus' name, we are blessed too. Giving is inherently therapeutic because in giving we receive. Isn't that just like God? When we offer ourselves to be used by Him, He blesses us too.

Enjoy leading this group, and watch for God to work deeply and powerfully in each step along the way. People in the group will be challenged and inspired, and they will wrestle with their own hurts and doubts more deeply than ever before. Don't be afraid of this struggle. It's an essential part of their preparation to *experience* God's love and strength as they learn to *express* those life-changing qualities to others around them. And watch as God uses them in incredible ways to transform lives.

SESSION PLANS

The facilitator should develop a plan for scheduling the study, providing promotional materials, personally enlisting participants, arranging for the meeting room, ordering member books, and supplying other materials.

The most important part of having a successful study as a group is prayer, prayer, and more prayer. Encourage participants to pray with and for each other throughout the study.

A second essential is knowing God's Word. Each week begins with a Bible verse. Encourage your participants to memorize the verse. Memory card reminders are listed on page 159. Suggest that learners carry the verse in their wallet or purse, refer to it several times during the week, and be prepared to say it aloud with the others in the next session. No one need be embarrassed as you say it together.

INTRODUCTION SESSION (OPTIONAL)

Before the Session

1. Skim the member book as much as you can before the introduction session. Pay particular attention to the first seven pages.
2. Provide name tags (optional), pencils or pens, Bibles, and an attendance roster.
3. Order a member book for each participant. Couples each need their own member books. Allow two to three weeks for delivery.
4. Some groups will pay for their own member books. If this is your plan, provide a container for checks or cash and remind those who were not prepared to bring payment to the next group meeting.

During the Session

1. Because this study may be intimidating to some people, begin with a game. Have persons lined up on two facing walls. Name one wall *yes* and the other *no* with your hand motion (or attach a sign to each wall). As you read the following statements ask members to move from wall to wall to communicate that the statement best reflects their answer.
   - When I hear about a death in the church family, I'm usually the first one to visit the grieved relatives.
   - I don't wait for someone to ask me. I look for ways to help other people.
   - I'm comfortable visiting in a hospital.
   - I'm comfortable visiting in a nursing home.
   - Praying with others is not hard for me.
   - My Bible goes with me wherever I go. I can usually find a helpful passage to read.

   As members walk back and forth according to their answers, hopefully they will see that they are not alone in needing some training.
2. Describe the intention of this study by paraphrasing from the Introduction and from week one. Say: *This training will help you with your relational skills. You experience the challenges of being a friend almost every day in your job, neighborhood, home, or church. You will learn some new skills and be a more effective friend if you follow the steps laid out in this book.*
3. Use emotional language to challenge participants to have a heart for hurting people (compassion, grace, forgiveness, mercy, etc.). Read Matthew 5:3-12. Ask: *Which characteristics mentioned by Jesus would describe a trusted friend?* List responses on a writing surface such as a marker board, poster, or tear sheet.
4. Brainstorm how this study could be used in your church. Possible answers include:
   - as a small group or Bible study
   - to train group leaders for women's and men's ministries
   - to train deacons

- to train all small group leaders in the church
- to train all ministry leaders in the church
- as an open class and invite the whole church to come

5. Brainstorm how this study could help you be a better
   - Small-group leader
   - Sunday School teacher
   - Deacon
   - Spouse of staff member
   - Women's ministry leader
   - Men's ministry leader
   - Other_____

6. As time permits, walk participants through the book, pointing out the authors, weeks of study, Appendix, and memory refresher cards. Assign the Introduction and Week 1 for the next group meeting.

7. If you have decided to use the Scripture memory approach, have members turn to page 9 and read the memory verse for Week 1 together. Explain that although it is long in terms of words, it is easy to learn by paraphrasing the message:

   I praise God because He has comforted me.
   Therefore, I can comfort others in any
      trouble with that same comfort I received.

   Point out the verse on page 9. Instruct learners to tear or cut out the verse as a refresher card for their purse or wallet.

8. Close in prayer, thanking God for the comfort He gives to believers.

WEEK 1
CARING FOR PEOPLE IN NEED

Before the Session

1. Continue to bring extra pens or pencils and Bibles. Name tags are optional from this session forward.

2. Provide opportunity for payment of the books.

3. Read and complete the learning activities in Week 1. Select ideas or examples that have significance to you. Be prepared to discuss them in the group.

4. Read "Traditions of Christian Care" on page 120 in the Appendix. In the context of history, this article helps people see that caring for others is the model set in the New Testament that has continued throughout Christian history. Especially relevant is the work of the Puritans as "physicians of the soul."

5. Display a poster with the three group assignments in Step 9 of the session plan.

6. If you did not have an introduction session, look over the plan to discover any information that you may need to share in this session.

During the Session

1. Welcome members and introduce any new members to the group.

2. Ask someone to lead in prayer for today's study.

3. Together recite 2 Corinthians 1:3-4.

4. Ask members to call out a word or phrase to describe their reaction to the content of Week 1. Use a popcorn style where everyone calls out the first words that come to mind. Capture as many of these as you can using an available writing surface.

5. Based on these comments, spend some time reflecting on these "first impressions." Seek to reassure, explain, and give insights as needed.

6. Ask: *Why does this study refer to trusted friends and not to counselors? Is our church a "safe place" to share our hurts and needs?*

7. Instruct members to turn to page 120 and read aloud or paraphrase the words you found helpful in the traditions of Christian counseling in the church. Discuss implications for your church. Suggest that members read the article in detail after the session.

8. Ask: *Which of the case studies throughout Week 1 most appealed to you? Have you had a similar experience?*

9. Form groups of two or more persons. Ask each group to determine in their opinion:
   a. the strongest biblical mandate to be trusted friends (pp. 16-18)
   b. the goal of becoming trusted friends (pp. 20-21)
   c. their reactions to the learning activity following the foundational principles (pp. 21-24)

10. After reports, review the characteristics of trusted friends. Brainstorm suggestions for future training and resources needed to become trusted friends in your congregation. List these on a writing surface.

11. Turn to page 29 and read the memory verse for Week 2. Instruct members to tear or cut the refresher card for use during the week.

12. Close with prayer that you would grow in ways that would make each person a better trusted friend.

WEEK 2
SHOWING WE CARE

Before the Session

1. Read and complete the learning activities in Week 2. Select ideas or examples that have significance to you. Mark learning activities that would be good discussion starters.

2. Read pages 121-127 in the Appendix. Be prepared to review the first two stages of grief.

3. Model "hiding God's word in your heart" by memorizing the verse for Week 2 (see Ps. 119:11).

4. Bring blank sheets of paper and pens or pencils for the opening activity.

During the Session

1. Welcome members and lead in prayer.

2. Recite together the memory verse for Week 2.

3. Give each person a blank sheet of paper. Ask learners to list the names or events that are currently of concern to your church family. These will not be read aloud or collected. Allow one minute to write.

4. Ask members to call out the number of incidents or people they knew about. Average the numbers. Ask: *Does the number indicate a need for a trusted friend ministry?* Say: *In Week 2 we read that "truth is most powerfully and fully absorbed if it is modeled and caught by a trusted friend who cares deeply about the hurting person."*

5. Invite a volunteer to review the short-term model of care recommended for trusted friends. Ask: *How should trusted friends relate to the pastor and staff?* Then ask the group to define Christ-centered counseling. Record the statement on a writing surface.

6. Select volunteers to tell what they wrote in response to the questions under "Previewing the Process" (pp. 32-35). Encourage those

who did not answer the questions to take notes as others share. Seek to correct an answer that might not be the best in that situation without being critical of the responder.

7. Briefly review the four steps in a crisis situation. Suggest members turn to pages 122-124 in the Appendix while you explain and illustrate the first two stages of grief. Ask the group to recall examples of these stages from previous experiences.

8. As a group, answer the learning activity at the bottom of page 40.

9. Enlist a different person to explain why each of the misconceptions listed on pages 42-44 are incorrect.

10. Explain that growth in pointing people to Christ and helping them grow in their faith is a process we will experience with each other as well as with hurting people. As a group activity lead members to identify ways they can grow in each area of the eight keys.

11. Direct the group's attention to the memory verse for Week 3. Instruct members to use the card on page 159 as a reminder to learn the verse.

12. Invite a volunteer to close with prayer.

WEEK 3
BECOMING A GREAT LISTENER

Before the Session

1. In this session we will introduce the idea of referring people we encounter to counselors, community agencies, and other sources of help. Be prepared to contribute ideas to the list on page 62.

2. If you have not finished reading the member book, glance ahead at the sections in Weeks 5 and 6 on putting together a referral directory.

3. Read and complete the learning activities in Week 3. Select ideas or examples that have significance to you. Mark learning activities that would be good discussion starters.

4. Read pages 123-125 in the Appendix. Be prepared to review the last three stages of grief.

During the Session

1. Welcome members and lead in prayer.

2. Recite together the memory verse for Week 3. Ask: *How can listening well affect your words and actions?*

3. Ask: *Who would you nominate for "world's best listener"? Why?* Allow multiple responses.

4. On a writing surface ask members to list reasons why communication is so complex. Brainstorm reasons why listening is complex.

5. Compare the way Dwayne initiated conversation with Rob to Jesus' conversation with the crippled man in John 5:1-9. Make the point that often we assume we know why a person is acting strangely, becoming quiet, or appearing angry. We must never prejudge a situation. Ask: *If you prejudged someone's problem, how would that affect your listening to the person?*

6. Under the heading "Attending," review the three bolded elements listed by the authors.

Invite volunteers to share which would be the hardest aspect for them to do consistently.

7. Select a volunteer to explain the problem with *why* questions. Then choose a creative member to act out several nonverbal signals and let the group guess the feeling that is being conveyed.

8. As a group, share answers to the question on the benefits of silence (p. 54).

9. Ask volunteers to share what they wrote in response to the prompts on mirroring emotions on page 55.

10. Draw a T-bar chart on a writing surface. Label the left side *compare* and the right side *contrast*. Invite comparisons and contrasts to the way Jesus confronted the women in John 4:1-26 and John 8:1-11. List each answer on the chart. Then remind members that we often treat people and their problems with a cookie cutter mentality. We must focus on the person at hand and erase our well-rehearsed scripts with all the easy answers.

11. Introduce the group to the assignment to compile a resource directory for your church by the end of Week 6. (If earlier groups have compiled one, add to it or double-check it for current information.) Ask them to begin by telling the group what they wrote on page 62 from each other's experiences. Ask someone with a laptop computer to record these during the week for use in the directory.

12. Affirm the importance of confidentiality and humility from the material in Week 3.

13. Ask: *What role would grief play when you are seeking to listen to others?* Then invite members to turn to page 126 in the Appendix. As they follow along, explain the last three stages of grief, with emphasis on listening skills.

14. Close with prayer, thanking God for always being willing to listen to us as we pray.

WEEK 4
SCRIPTURES AND PRAYER

Before the Session

1. Some of the group may find it incredulous that a person might not want to hear a Bible verse or a prayer for his or her situation. Or a person might allow it without wanting it. Seek to understand why this reaction occurs so that you can deal with this issue in Week 4.

2. Read and complete the learning activities in Week 4. Select ideas or examples that have significance to you. Mark learning activities that would be good discussion starters.

3. Pre-enlist someone in the group or a person who is not in the group to share their testimony of how God uses pain and waiting as His "curriculum" (p. 70).

4. Read pages 128-129 in the Appendix. Be prepared to make assignments to a pair or small group to read the verses for one of the topics.

5. Bring gospel tracts and other witnessing materials. Be prepared to demonstrate the ABC method.

During the Session

1. Welcome members and lead in prayer.

2. Recite together the memory verse for Week 4. Ask: *What does it teach us about the Bible?*

3. Read James 1:2-4. Invite volunteers to read their responses to the learning activity on page 69.

4. Ask for reactions to the psalms of David used in Week 5. Be prepared with your observations.

5. Share with the group Scriptures God has used to help you be honest about pain and disappointment, as well as thankfulness and praise (p. 76). Then ask other volunteers to share their thoughts.

leader guide

151

6. Give a short lecture on the patterns of prayer (pp. 80-81). Ask: *Does God answer every prayer?* After several responses, ask for ways He answers prayer (yes, no, later, when you've grown from this experience, etc.).

7. Review Daniel 9, setting the stage for the appearance of the angel Gabriel in verse 20. Ask: *What can we learn from verse 23?* (We may not know our prayers have been answered until God shows us.)

8. Refer to the "Passages of Encouragement and Hope" in the Appendix (pp. 128-129). Ask them to become familiar with key passages that might be easily recalled in an appropriate setting.

9. Select four people to explain one of the statements about our identity in Christ (pp. 78-79).

10. Spend the remainder of the time discussing ways to share Christ with nonbelievers. Distribute several tracts. Teach the ABC plan as well. It is located on page 142 in the Leader Guide.

11. Close with prayer that the group will be more faithful prayer warriors, especially as they serve as trusted friends.

WEEK 5
RESOURCES AND REFERRALS

Before the Session

1. Read and complete the learning activities in Week 5. Select ideas or examples that have significance to you. Mark learning activities that would be good discussion starters.

2. Read pages 130-133 in the appendix. Be prepared to review "Why People Struggle and Suffer." As much as possible, relate these people and situations to opportunities for referral.

3. Check with your pastor/staff or other church leader to update him or her to your progress on the referral directory. Make it clear that the directory will need to be approved by someone in authority over you before it is bound or put in a notebook and available to all.

4. Since the referral directory should be finished at the end of session 6, you may want to assign spots that still need to be filled to individuals or pairs. Their additions would be given during session 6. If you feel the information you have will be sufficient—or sufficient after session 6—you don't need to make outside assignments.

5. Consider how you want to use the case studies in Week 6. You may want to preassign them to pairs or trios at the end of session 5 so they can put thought into their responses.

6. Ask the member with the laptop computer to bring it to the session to compile the additional names in the referral directory.

During the Session

1. Welcome members and lead in prayer.

2. Recite together the memory verse for Week 5. Point out that although it was written to pastors, we can learn from their example as shepherds to show humility in the roles God asks us to play.

3. Ask if anyone has been a trusted friend to someone this week. If so, help them debrief the experience. Allow other group members to give their feedback also. Then ask: *What information and/or skills set found in this resource were used in this encounter?* Have in mind one of your own experiences in case no one responds with an example. Debrief as above.

4. Assign one of the common problems to each pair or individual. Ask them to review the material found on pages 86-93 for the insights about how to be a trusted friend to each kind of individual as they face these varied problems.

5. Encourage the group to turn to the case study of Alice and Beth. Use their experience as an example of the short-term model recommended in session 2.

6. Call attention to the steps to referring someone to a professional on pages 94-97. Ask: *After the person makes an appointment with a referral source, what should be your role?*

7. Spend the remainder of the time collecting new sources members found since Week 3. Ask the person with a computer to add these as they are voiced. As a group add additional information beside each name such as the list of information on pages 97-98.

8. Close with prayer asking God to bless this directory and use it to His glory.

WEEK 6
GETTING STARTED

Before the Session

1. Read and complete the learning activities in Week 6. Select ideas or examples that have significance to you. Mark learning activities that would be good discussion starters.

2. Read pages 139-141 in the Appendix. Be prepared to review the issue of confidentiality.

During the Session

1. Welcome members and lead in prayer.

2. Recite together the memory verse for Week 6. Ask: *Do we work for a reward? Then why would it matter to you? (We want to please those we love.)*

3. Assign the case studies to individuals, pairs, or groups. Ask each group to report in five to seven minutes.

4. Afterward, if you have persons who enjoy a role play, have the group make up a scenario and the people involved. Give the actors a few minutes to make up their script. A role play can also be set up with obvious errors for the group to list afterward. Always debrief a role-play so that learning takes place and affirm (no criticism allowed) the actors for their willingness to participate.

5. As time allows, point out the limitations of a trusted friend and review the issue of confidentiality in the Appendix.

6. Spend the remaining moments on the questions at the end of Week 6.

7. Consider a follow-up session in three to six weeks both to update or share concerns with the directory and to help each other as they meet hurting persons. Enforce the rule of confidentiality.

8. Thank the participants before closing in prayer.

ADDITIONAL

WOMEN REACHING WOMEN IN CRISIS

Women all across the nation are experiencing the crippling pain that results from walking through a crisis situation in their lives.

The greater tragedy is they are walking through these shadows alone, afraid there is no hope and no one will understand. *Women Reaching Women in Crisis* is a powerful downloadable resource that provides help in recognizing and dealing with women experiencing one or more crises that have become all to common, even in our churches. The series provides issue-specific information and ministering guidance, and leaders can learn about the symptoms of each crisis, as well as discover some of the treatment options and how to find professional help while supporting women through these overwhelming situations.

Also available in this online series is an Introductory Handbook. This essential resource provides critical information for helping the women's leader recognize crisis situations that require more expertise than she can provide, identify referral sources in the community, and develop the skills to make professional counseling referrals.

Online Handbooks include:

Crisis Introduction | 005034986   Sexual Addiction | 005034985
Prodigal Children | 005034983   Substance Abuse | 005034980
Depression | 005034984   Domestic Abuse | 005034981

- Developed by leading women's counselors
- Downloadable handbooks provide immediate help
- Addresses 5 of the most common crisis situations women face
- Equips women's leaders with the tools to engage with and call women in crisis out of isolation
- Integrates Biblical teachings with proven counseling practices
- Builds confidence in women's leaders to offer help to other women in need

A Must Have for Women's Ministry Leaders, Teachers, Class Leaders, Small-Group Leaders & Coordinators

RESOURCES

PICKING UP THE PIECES

REAL HELP FOR REAL PEOPLE LIVING REAL LIFE.

As our hearts engage in an epic battle, there are times we suffer deep, debilitating wounds. How do we make sense of these times and reconcile the reality of our pain with the goodness of God? At other times, we've just lost touch with our hearts, knowing there must be more but not sure how to find it. It is in both these places that God is able to touch our hearts and redeem the shame and failures of our lives. Whenever you struggle, God's heart aches for you. He desperately wants to walk with you through your struggles and lead you to hope, healing and freedom. *Picking Up the Pieces* is a series of honest, experiential Bible studies that will help you in the journey to recover your heart!

- Written by leading therapists and members of the American Association of Christian Counselors
- Honest, experiential Bible studies that will set captives free from destructive patterns
- Probing questions for your heart and God to help bind up the broken places
- Unique journaling exercises at the end of each session to help understand how God really feels about you
- Replaces beauty for the ashes of shame and failure

Experience the power of healing in a new and fresh way with redemptive music from *Picking Up the Pieces.*

GREAT RESOURCE FOR:

- Support Groups
- Recovery Groups
- Small Groups
- Church Classes
- Accountability Groups
- Counseling Centers

Start your own *Picking Up the Pieces* ministry with this complete book on launching soul care in your church by Dr. Chuck Hannaford.

- Identify the key areas of need in your church
- Develop leaders capable of restoring hope to hurting people
- Understand the needs that often go unspoken
- Discover ways to develop real authenticity and trust and expose the masks people wear

"I remember the feeling of freedom I received from the group's willingness to share their lives through the questions and discussion provoked by your study. Thank you for helping lift the darkness from my life."

SANDRA K. HOY

TITLE	ISBN	PRICE	SESSIONS
BOOK STUDIES			
Redeeming the Tears: A Journey Through Grief and Loss	1574941860	$7.99	8
Stop the Madness: Finding Freedom From Addictions	1574941879	$8.99	13
Recovering from Divorce: Overcoming the Death of a Dream	1574942220	$7.99	8
Radical Reconciliation: The Journey of Forgiveness	1574942212	$7.99	8
The Secret Seductress: Pulling the Plug on Porn	1574942239	$7.99	8
Surrendering the Secret: Healing the Heartbreak of Abortion	1574943052	$7.99	8
HANDBOOK			
Picking Up the Pieces Handbook: Create A Dynamic Soul Care Ministry	1574943448	$12.99	–
REDEMPTIVE MUSIC			
Pursued By God: An Experience in Redemptive Worship	1574942921	$14.98	–
Somebody's Daughter: Confronting the Lies of Pornography	157494360X	$14.98	–

Building community one group at a time.

WWW.SERENDIPITYHOUSE.COM · 800.525.9563

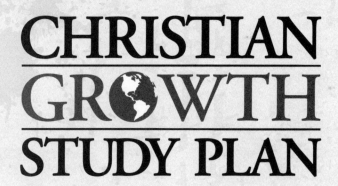

CHRISTIAN GROWTH STUDY PLAN

In the Christian Growth Study Plan, this book *Trusted Friend* is a resource for course credit in the subject area Personal Life of the Christian Growth category of plans. To receive credit, read the book, complete the learning activities, show your work to your pastor, a staff member or church leader, then complete the following information. This page may be duplicated. Send the completed page to:

Christian Growth Study Plan
One LifeWay Plaza, Nashville, TN 37234-0117
FAX: (615)251-5067
E-mail: cgspnet@lifeway.com

For information about the Christian Growth Study Plan, refer to the Christian Growth Study Plan Catalog. It is located online at www.lifeway.com/cgsp. If you do not have access to the Internet, contact the Christian Growth Study Plan office (1.800.968.5519) for the specific plan you need for your ministry.

TRUSTED FRIEND
COURSE NUMBER: CG–1101

PARTICIPANT INFORMATION

Social Security Number (USA ONLY-optional) | Personal CGSP Number* | Date of Birth (MONTH, DAY, YEAR)

Name (First, Middle, Last) | Home Phone

Address (Street, Route, or P.O. Box) | City, State, or Province | Zip/Postal Code

Email Address for CGSP use

Please check appropriate box: ❑ Resource purchased by church ❑ Resource purchased by self ❑ Other

CHURCH INFORMATION

Church Name

Address (Street, Route, or P.O. Box) | City, State, or Province | Zip/Postal Code

CHANGE REQUEST ONLY

❑ Former Name

❑ Former Address | City, State, or Province | Zip/Postal Code

❑ Former Church | City, State, or Province | Zip/Postal Code

Signature of Pastor, Conference Leader, or Other Church Leader | Date

*New participants are requested but not required to give SS# and date of birth. Existing participants, please give CGSP# when using SS# for the first time. Thereafter, only one ID# is required. **Mail to:** Christian Growth Study Plan, One LifeWay Plaza, Nashville, TN 37234-0117. Fax: (615)251-5067.

Revised 4-05

WEEK 1

"For the word of God is living and active. Sharper than any double-edged sword, it penetrates even to dividing soul and spirit, joints and marrow; it judges the thoughts and attitudes of the heart. Nothing in all creation is hidden from God's sight. Everything is uncovered and laid bare before the eyes of him to whom we must give account." *Hebrews 4:12-13*

WEEK 2

"Be shepherds of God's flock that is under your care, serving as overseers— not because you must, but because you are willing, as God wants you to be ... not lording it over those entrusted to you, but being examples to the flock." *1 Peter 5:2,3*

WEEK 3

"Whatever you do, work at it with all your heart, as working for the Lord, not for men, since you know that you will receive an inheritance from the Lord as a reward."
Colossians 3:23-24

WEEK 4

"Praise be to the God ... who comforts us in all our troubles, so that we can comfort those in any trouble with the comfort we ourselves have received from God."
2 Corinthians 1:3,4

WEEK 5

"He who walks with the wise grows wise, but a companion of fools suffers harm."
Proverbs 13:20

WEEK 6

"My dear brothers, take note of this: Everyone should be quick to listen, slow to speak and slow to become angry."
James 1:19